LITTLE WOMEN

THE OFFICIAL MOVIE COMPANION

✳

LITTLE WOMEN

THE OFFICIAL MOVIE COMPANION

GINA MCINTYRE

PHOTOS BY WILSON WEBB

ABRAMS BOOKS FOR YOUNG READERS
NEW YORK

CHAPTER ONE

LOUISA MAY ALCOTT

AND THE LEGACY OF *LITTLE WOMEN*

✻

*"I do think that families are
the most beautiful things
in all the world!"*

—JO MARCH

Jo March, as played by Saoirse Ronan, at her writing desk

Ever the writer, Jo puts pen to page at the boarding house

LIKE ALL THE BEST STORIES, THIS one has humble beginnings: at a small, hand-fashioned desk affixed to the windowsill of a second-floor bedroom in a ramshackle house in Concord, Massachusetts. Built in the 1600s, the home was in poor condition when philosopher and educator Amos Bronson Alcott bought the residence for his family nearly two centuries later, in 1857. Yet one of the world's most enduring literary masterpieces was written inside its modest walls.

Louisa May Alcott's semiautobiographical novel *Little Women, or, Meg, Jo, Beth, and Amy* was an immediate sensation upon its publication in 1868 and has remained a towering classic for decades. In 150 years, not only has the book never gone out of print, but it has been translated into upwards of fifty languages. In 2016, *Little Women* was named one of *Time*'s top 100 young adult books of all time,

and some accounts suggest that more than ten million copies of the book have been sold.

Readers the world over remain riveted by Alcott's tenderly rendered depiction of life in nineteenth-century New England, where the fictional March family resides. Their accommodations might be modest, but their home is overflowing with love. Sisters Meg, Jo, Beth, and Amy live together with their adored mother, Marmee. With their father called to serve in the Civil War and their family fortune depleted, the women have few luxuries. Nevertheless, their lives are full and happy, sustained by mutual admiration and respect and the comfort they find in each other's company.

Alcott's novel details the pivotal years in the March sisters' lives as they make their way from adolescence into adulthood, and in writing the book, she brought many of her own experiences to the page. She herself served as the model for headstrong Jo, the boyish girl who cares passionately about her writing and vows never to marry for fear of losing her autonomy. Alcott's sisters, Anna, Lizzie, and May, inspired Jo's siblings, each a well-drawn character in her own right. And just like the March girls, the Alcott women worshipped their mother, Abigail or "Abba," whom they called Marmee.

Their father was a more complicated figure. He espoused progressive ideals about equality and maintained close friendships with writers Ralph Waldo Emerson and Henry David Thoreau, key voices in the Transcendentalist movement. Bronson Alcott lived a peripatetic existence, moving his family more than thirty times. He also founded a short-lived utopian community called Fruitlands, where residents bathed in cold water and ate only vegetables that grew above the ground. When the society collapsed after less than a year, Bronson opted not to pursue gainful employment, leaving the family largely destitute.

It was under these circumstances that Alcott began penning thrillers under the pseudonym A. M. Barnard, selling them to local weekly publications (titles included "Pauline's Passion and Punishment") and bringing in much-needed income. Eventually, her publisher asked her to write a tale that would appeal to girls. Her own home provided plenty of material. She has been quoted as saying that she "never liked girls or knew many, except my sisters; but our queer plays and experiences may prove interesting, though I doubt it."

When *Little Women* opens, the March girls are knitting in the twilight, preparing for their first Christmas without their father. Meg, the oldest at sixteen, strikes a "complaining tone," saddened by the fact that the family's meager circumstances have forced her to find work as a governess. Equally cross

Jo March, played by actor Saoirse Ronan, prepares to enter the boarding house

Saoirse Ronan discusses a scene with director Greta Gerwig

is fifteen-year-old Jo, short for Josephine, "a bookworm" who bemoans the fact that she wasn't a born a boy who could go and fight herself. Peacemaker Beth, a mature thirteen, suggests that washing dishes might be the worst work in the world, because it keeps her from practicing music. Young Amy, twelve, believes she is the most aggrieved, however, what with her entirely unsatisfactory nose and her inability to buy the new drawing pencils she so strongly desires.

Whatever affectionate sisterly quarrels might arise among the Marches, their loyalty each other, and to their mother, is fierce and unwavering, though Jo's ferocity might be the most steadfast trait of all. Of her family, she is the least interested in abiding by the rules of civil society. She longs only to invent wild plays or spend her hours writing in the confines of the attic that doubles as her study. She finds an unruly kindred spirit in the wealthy young man whose majestic house sits across the way—orphaned Theodore Laurence, who resides in empty opulence with his emotion-

ally distant grandfather. Laurie, or Teddy as she calls him, becomes Jo's closest friend and confidante, a mischievous soul mate whose love for the wild girl knows no bounds.

Jo stood apart as a singular heroine: angrily defiant, headstrong, and boldly clinging to youth rather than succumbing to adulthood and its expectations that women surrender their independence and live instead for their husbands and children. She was a transformative figure for readers who might never have dared to dream of a creative career, or, in fact, any career at all. In an interview for the Harry Potter films, author J. K. Rowling said: "It is hard to overstate what she meant to a small, plain girl called Jo, who had a hot temper and a burning ambition to be a writer." Among the other luminaries who have declared their affinity for Jo: Gloria Steinem, Gertrude Stein, Simone de Beauvoir, Hillary Rodham Clinton, national poet laureate Tracy K. Smith, novelist Ann Petry, Supreme Court justices Sandra Day O'Connor and Ruth Bader Ginsberg, and rock icon Patti Smith.

GREET ADAPTATIONS

LOUISA MAY ALCOTT'S BELOVED NOVEL HAS BEEN TOLD AND RETOLD COUNTLESS TIMES. HERE'S A PRIMER ON THE VARIOUS INCARNATIONS OF THE TIMELESS TALE.

ON THE BIG SCREEN

Ruby Miller was the first actor to play Jo in the first movie adaptation of Alcott's classic, though her performance in the British silent film has been lost to time. One year later, Dorothy Bernard took a turn in the lead role in a US silent production. But it was the 1933 black-and-white production directed by George Cukor that might be the most memorable early version. It stars Katharine Hepburn as the headstrong protagonist, won an Oscar for its screenplay, and was nominated for best picture and best director. In 1949, Hollywood revisited the novel once more, this time in Technicolor with then thirty-one-year-old June Allyson as the fifteen-year-old Jo and a young Elizabeth Taylor in a blond wig as Amy. In 1994, Winona Ryder was nominated for best actress for her turn as Jo in the Gillian Armstrong–directed film.

ON THE STAGE

Little Women opened on Broadway for the first time on October 14, 1912, with a script written by Marian de Forest and actor Marie Pavey cast in the role of Jo. Decades later, in 2005, Sutton Foster reprised the role in a Virginia Theatre production with a book by Allan Knee, music by Jason Howland, and lyrics by Mindy Dickstein. Foster was nominated for a Tony Award for her performance. Composer and librettist Mark Adamo tried his hand at retelling *Little Women*, crafting an opera that opened to wide acclaim in 1998. Since then, various iterations of the production have played across the United States and in faraway destinations including Mexico, Australia, and Israel.

ON TELEVISION

Little Women's history on television dates to a 1939 NBC production of the 1912 Broadway play; it, along with a 1946 version, is considered lost. A 1958 musical version cut the story down to an hour and omitted one of the novel's landmark moments, Beth's tragic demise. The BBC has staged several *Little Women* productions over the years: The first aired in 1950; a nine-part series plagued by poor production values and performances aired in 1970; and most recently, a two-night, three-hour version aired in 2017 starring Maya Hawke as Jo. (The prize for most intriguing cast goes to a 1978 two-part American adaptation featuring *The Partridge Family* actor Susan Dey as Jo and William Shatner as Professor Bhaer.) In the 1980s, two anime versions were produced in Japan, where *Little Women* remains one of most widely read books among young girls.

Saoirse Ronan's Jo March and Laura Dern's
Marmee pore over pages of Jo's writing on set

A LITERARY LIFE

1832

Louisa May Alcott is born on November 29 in Germantown, Pennsylvania, the second child in what will become a family of four sisters.

1834

The Alcott family moves to Boston; Bronson Alcott opens the progressive Temple School, which closes six years later.

1843

Alcott moves with her family to Fruitlands, the Utopian commune founded in Harvard, Massachusetts, by her father and Charles Lane. It lasts from May through December.

1854

Alcott publishes a collection of original fairy tales and poems, *Flower Fables*.

1857

The Alcotts move to Orchard House.

1858

Alcott's younger sister, Lizzie Alcott, dies at the age of 22.

1860

Alcott's eldest sister, Anna, marries John Bridge Pratt at Orchard House; their sons, Frederick and John, later became the models for Demi and Daisy Brooke in *Little Women*.

1862

Alcott serves as a nurse at the Union Hotel Hospital in Georgetown, Virginia; she returns home the following year after contracting typhoid pneumonia. Although she seems near death, she ultimately makes a hard-fought recovery.

1863

Writing under the pseudonym A. M. Barnard, Alcott publishes the story "Pauline's Passion and Punishment," in *Frank Leslie's Illustrated Newspaper*. She is paid one hundred dollars.

1863

Alcott publishes *Hospital Sketches*, inspired by her service as a Civil War nurse. An enormous success, the work sees Alcott find her voice writing "reality fiction." The volume helps turn Alcott into an in-demand writer.

1864

Alcott writes *Moods* about a tomboy seeking adventure who marries the wrong man.

1869

The second volume of *Little Women* is published, allowing Alcott to answer what became of the March sisters.

1868

Alcott publishes the first volume of *Little Women* after Thomas Niles, of Roberts Brothers publishers, asks her to write a story for girls.

1871

Another follow-up, *Little Men*, is published to strong sales.

1875

A committed suffragette, like her mother, Alcott attends the Women's Congress of 1875 in Syracuse, New York.

1879

Alcott becomes the first woman to cast a vote in a school board election in Concord.

1886

The final book featuring heroine Jo March, *Jo's Boys*, is published.

1888

Alcott dies, two days after her father, on March 4 at age fifty-five. She is buried with her sisters in Sleepy Hollow Cemetery in Concord.

Told more through a collection of moving, detailed episodes than a grand, driving narrative, Alcott's novel was revolutionary for its authentic depiction of the lives of young girls, their concerns, their aspirations, and their imperfections. The first print run of *Little Women* numbered some two thousand copies. It sold out in days, becoming a runaway literary sensation beyond anything Alcott might have imagined. She was then asked to augment her original twenty-three chapters, so she came up with a second volume, published in 1869, which brought the story to a more natural, if unexpected, conclusion.

Meg and John get married—though married life proves difficult for the young couple, who grapple with financial hardship—and have spirited twins. Amy travels to Europe with Aunt Carroll to further her study of art and briefly considers marrying wealthy English suitor Fred Vaughn in pursuit of a comfortable life. In volume one, Beth had contracted scarlet fever after visiting the family's ailing, poverty-stricken neighbors, the Hummels. Although she made a preliminary recovery, her health is never fully restored, and death hovers at the margins of her story before finally claiming her life.

Alcott's most controversial narrative choice, however, involved the fate of Laurie and Jo. Readers had longed for the two friends to wed and live together in bliss, but Alcott was reluctant for Jo to marry anyone. In *Little Women*'s second volume, Jo rejects Laurie's proposal, insisting that she is destined to remain alone all her days. Later, though, fate intervenes, and Jo does fall in love with and marry a much older German professor, Friedrich Bhaer, whose serious demeanor and admirable intellect wins her heart. Meanwhile, a dejected, lovesick Laurie heads to Europe and finds a bride—Jo's sister Amy.

"Jo should have remained a literary spinster but so many enthusiastic young ladies wrote to me clamorously demanding that she should marry Laurie, or somebody, that I didn't dare refuse & out of perversity went & made a funny match for her," Alcott wrote in a letter to a friend, explaining her choice. The novel concludes with Jo Bhaer having inherited the Plumfield estate from the family's wealthy benefactor, Aunt March, and establishing a school for boys with Friedrich.

Readers eagerly devoured the second volume of Alcott's saga, making her a wealthy woman who was in a unique position to provide for her beloved family. She continued writing about the adventures of the March clan, publishing a follow-up novel, *Little Men: Life at Plumfield with Jo's Boys* in 1871. Her next book, *Jo's Boys, and How They Turned Out: A Sequel to "Little Men,"* was released in 1886, two years before her death at age fifty-five. All proved tremendously popular, but *Little Women* has proven the most enduring; it's been adapted for virtually every medium, told and retold for each new generation.

What is most remarkable about her novel, written from the confines of her Concord, Massachusetts, home, is the way it can travel. Alcott's novel has reached across the centuries because of the profound way her writing captures the glories, joys, and depths of despair that we experience on the journey from adolescence to adulthood, the triumphs and tragedies that inform who we become. The book is both specific and universal, rooted in Alcott's personal experience yet able to speak to readers of all ages and from all walks of life. *Little Women* is a story for the ages.

TRANSCENDENTALISM

By the standards of the 1800s, the members of the Alcott family were progressive radicals: committed abolitionists, environmentalists, and strong proponents of equal rights for women. But they were not alone in their liberal ideals. Alcott's family belonged to a class of writers and thinkers known as the Transcendentalists; its most famous adherents include poet Ralph Waldo Emerson, author Henry David Thoreau, and journalist Margaret Fuller, whose book *Woman in the Nineteenth Century* is considered the first major feminist work in the United States.

A social movement that developed in New England in the early to mid-1800s, Transcendentalism held that divinity can be seen in all of nature and humanity. Its central text is *Walden*, Thoreau's account of the two years he spent living in a cabin on the north shore of Walden Pond, which lies just a few miles outside of Concord, not far from the Alcott family home.

From her earliest days, Louisa May Alcott was exposed to the principles espoused by the likes of Emerson and Thoreau, both of whom were frequent guests of her father during their years at Orchard House. Although she agreed with many of the movement's chief tenets, as with most things, Alcott preferred to go her own way. She would later publish a slightly fictionalized, satirical account of her time at her father's failed commune, Fruitlands, titled *Transcendental Wild Oats*. It wasn't necessarily a flattering portrait.

Still, Alcott carried with her a profound love and respect for nature all her days. That affection for the natural world comes through in passages from her journal, including the following:

"I had an early run in the woods before the dew was off the grass. The moss was like velvet, and as I ran under the arches of yellow and red leaves I sang for joy, my heart was so bright and the world so beautiful. I stopped at the end of the walk and saw the sunshine out over the wide 'Virginia meadows.'"

(Opposite) Jo and Laurie's triumphant first dance at the Gardiner's New Year's Eve party

CHAPTER TWO

NEW IMPRESSIONS—

GRETA GERWIG WRITES THE NEXT CHAPTER

✳

"Women have minds and souls as well as hearts, ambition and talent as well as beauty, and I'm sick of being told that love is all a woman is fit for."

—JO MARCH

Saoirse Ronan holds a prop letter in between takes

Cinematographer Yorick Le Saux on set with director Greta Gerwig

EACH GENERATION DESERVES ITS own *Little Women*.

That was the thinking of producers Amy Pascal, Robin Swicord, and Denise Di Novi when they decided to update Alcott's novel for a modern audience. Notably, it wasn't the first time the three Hollywood veterans had teamed up to translate the beloved novel for the screen. Swicord scripted and produced the 1994 version along with Di Novi for Sony Pictures, where Pascal was a high-ranking executive.

Directed by Australian filmmaker Gillian Armstrong, their first film was shot largely in Vancouver, British Columbia, with an all-star cast. Winona Ryder was nominated for an Oscar for her portrayal of Jo (the film's costume design and score were also nominated). The ensemble featured Trini Alvarado as Meg, Claire Danes as Beth, and Kirsten Dunst and Samantha Mathis both as Amy (Dunst por-trayed the younger incarnation of the char-acter), with Christian Bale as Laurie and Gabriel Byrne as Friedrich.

At the time of its release, critic Roger Ebert praised the film for underlining the larger themes inherent in Alcott's domestic drama: "It's a film about how all of life seems to stretch ahead of us when we're young, and how, through a series of choices, we narrow our destiny."

With the passage of time, however, Pascal felt there was an opportunity to examine the text with fresh eyes. Given the richness and depth of the book, the producers felt they could explore different facets of the lives of the Marches with a new film. "It's a different world now than it was when we made the movie before," says Pascal, who stepped down from her post as cochairman of Sony in 2015 to produce full-time. "The thing about the book is that it is much more satirical and knowing and much less sentimental than some of the adaptations have been. And I felt like this was a time where we could do a movie that was truer to the book and truer to Louisa May Alcott."

Swicord, whose credits include *Matilda* (1996), *Practical Magic* (1998), and *Memoirs of a Geisha* (2005), agreed that the time was right. "I do feel that every generation should have a chance to look again at the classic films that shaped their childhood and the classic books that shaped their childhood and say, 'What is here for our time?'" Swicord says. "We needed a certain kind of *Little Women* in 1994, and I feel the same is true for 2019. . . . We have to have stories in which we see ourselves and can come out of the theater thinking deeply about what it is to be female in the time that we're living."

It was Di Novi who suggested that Greta Gerwig might be the right person for a new adaptation. At the time, Gerwig was best known as an actor whose relatability and charm in such films as director Noah Baumbach's 2010 offbeat comedy *Greenberg* had made her a critical darling. She and Baumbach later struck up a writing partnership—Gerwig initially had been interested in a career as a playwright—and their first collaboration, the comedy *Frances Ha*, starred Gerwig as a New York woman who apprentices with a dance company.

"I had loved her as an [actor], but when I saw her screenplay for *Frances Ha*, I thought she had such a specific and deep intimacy with the female experience and a fearlessness in terms of being vulnerable and authentic—

Emma Watson, Greta Gerwig, Saoirse Ronan, and Florence Pugh on set

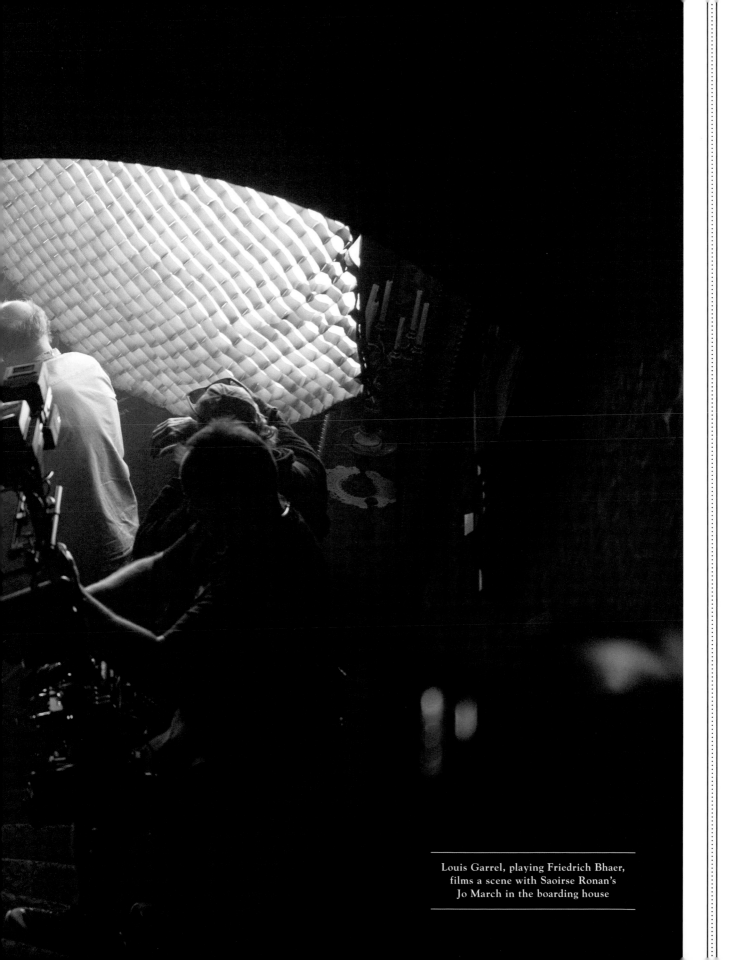

Louis Garrel, playing Friedrich Bhaer,
films a scene with Saoirse Ronan's
Jo March in the boarding house

that, to me, is what the Jo character embodies," Di Novi says. "Even though it was written at a time when women were so restricted and so constrained, Louisa May Alcott was able to create this character that was so free and so open and did not filter herself, did not dimin-

Greta Gerwig directs a scene in the schoolroom

ish herself. I saw that in Greta's work, that fearlessness, that authenticity and the courage to speak your truth."

Gerwig leapt at the opportunity. She had fallen in love with Alcott's novel when she was a girl and felt an incredible kinship with Jo March. "Jo felt like my heroine," Gerwig says. "She was the one I wanted to be like and was like, I suppose, in some ways. She seemed to have stature and that was thrilling."

Gerwig had a very specific point of view on the ideas at the heart of Alcott's novel, inspired in part by Virginia Woolf's assertion, "Intellectual freedom depends upon material things." "This book is a book about money, and why is it so hard for women to get it," Gerwig says. "The first lines of the book are 'Christmas

won't be Christmas without any presents. It's so dreadful to be poor. I don't think it's fair that some girls have lots of pretty things and some girls have nothing at all.' The circumstances of women not being able to earn their own living is everywhere in it."

"Louisa May Alcott, she was one of those people that I think pulled us into the next century," Gerwig adds. "The twentieth century was reaching down through her and giving her some ability to say, 'We're going to do this differently moving forward for women.' I don't know that *she* even understood it completely, but for me that economic piece of being an artist, being a woman, and dealing with money was so much of that entire narrative pulsing underneath the book."

She also felt strongly about how the sisters should be depicted on-screen. Specifically, she was interested in changing the perception of Amy from the pampered diva of the March clan—a girl more concerned with the shape of her nose than with the more serious interests of her sisters—into an assertive woman unafraid to pursue what she wanted from life. "I wanted her to be a worthy adversary for Jo," Gerwig says. "She and Jo are the two that have the biggest, brightest, craziest ambition. She has her eye on the door the whole time the way Jo does. She even has a line in the book, 'The world is hard on ambitious girls.' Often, Amy is played as being a bit prissy, and she's anything but. She's a monster. She wants to be the best artist in the world. That part of Amy is the same as Jo."

Pascal and the other producers were impressed by Gerwig's fresh perspective and the passion with which she articulated her ideas. In 2014, they hired her to adapt the screenplay. "It was the force of her personality and her ideas that made us realize that there was probably nobody else who could tell the story the way that she could," Pascal says.

It wasn't the only script Gerwig was writing at the time, however. She'd also been working on *Lady Bird*, a coming-of-age tale set in 2002 Sacramento about a Catholic high school student desperate to break out of her lower-middle-class suburban life. For the story, Gerwig borrowed elements from her own life. She, too, had grown up in the California capital, attending an all-girls Catholic school and longing to find a creative outlet.

Irish actor Saoirse Ronan starred as Christine "Lady Bird" McPherson, a teen who has a difficult relationship with her mother, Marion (Laurie Metcalf), and finds herself floundering in her friendship with bestie Julie (Beanie Feldstein), whom she leaves behind for a new crowd. She meets an effortlessly cool but ultimately useless boy named Kyle, played by Timothée Chalamet, who briefly claims Lady Bird's affections but eventually breaks her heart.

The film opened in 2017 to rapturous reviews and went on to earn five Academy Award nominations; Gerwig became only the fifth woman ever to be nominated for best

director. *Lady Bird* proved to *Little Women*'s producing team that no one but Gerwig should direct their film. Her innate understanding of the complexities of female relationships, the sympathy with which she treats her characters,

Director Greta Gerwig at the helm

and the humor with which she approaches the absurdities of life all made her exactly the right filmmaker to bring Alcott's classic to the screen.

"She's got it all," Pascal says. "She's incredibly sophisticated about the way that she shoots. She's obviously a brilliant writer, and the way that she works with actors is like the best of them. She gets right inside the characters. She brings things out in people. She's incredibly patient. She knows exactly what she wants, and she had a vision for this movie that was completely her own."

It was clear from the start, too, that Gerwig would reteam with her *Lady Bird* stars Ronan and Chalamet in the all-important roles of Jo and Laurie. "We never really thought of anybody else except for Saoirse and Timothée to play those characters," Pascal says. "It just seemed obvious, not only because of their relationship on that movie but also who they are in the world, what wonderful actors they are, and how much we felt they could break each other's hearts."

A clapperboard calls action on set

The crew watches as Emma Watson's Meg March, Saoirse Ronan's Jo March,
Laura Dern's Marmee, and Bob Odenkirk's Father March film a scene

Gerwig says that, for her, Ronan was as much a creative partner as an actor playing a role. "I said this when we made *Lady Bird* together, and it's true of this one, too. She's the cocreator of these films in the sense that she's an author. It's not just that she's saying things I've written; she really creates what the thing is. I don't know any other way to describe it. Like all great actors, she's a great filmmaker."

The rest of the cast is no less impressive. Emma Watson was brought on to play Meg March alongside talented newcomers Eliza Scanlen and Florence Pugh, chosen for Beth and Amy, respectively. Laura Dern agreed to play Marmee; Bob Odenkirk, Father March; and Chris Cooper, Laurie's grandfather, Mr. Laurence. And legend Meryl Streep signed on to play Aunt March, the highly opinionated wealthy relative who has no compunction about sharing her feelings about the family of troublemakers.

That such an ensemble of A-listers would team up for the film is a testament to the source material and to Gerwig's reputation, according to Swicord. "Her deep acting background gives her the confidence to let actors take the lead and be messy and try things," she says. "There's a wrong idea that many directors have—somehow they're in control and they're kind of a puppeteer, and it's their job to get the actors to do things a certain way to match a sort of preimagined performance. Greta has tremendous strength as a director because she fearlessly lets actors do human behavior and find things. She knows how to encourage them, and at the same time, how to begin to shape their performance."

And if ever there was any doubt about a scene, a set, or the tenor of an emotional moment, the filmmakers always agreed on the signpost to look to for guidance: Alcott's indelible novel.

THE FIRST TIME I READ
LITTLE WOMEN

THE FILM'S THREE PRODUCERS SHARE THEIR MEMORIES OF THE NOVEL THAT
CHANGED THEIR PERSPECTIVE ON GROWING UP FEMALE

DENISE DI NOVI

"I was about ten when I read the book. It was a revelation to me that a girl, that a young woman, could be a writer and create something and have the courage to leave her family and go off and live in New York and dare to be different and have different interests and speak up for herself and get in trouble. She was such an inspiring character to me. The theme of the book and of Jo's story is finding her own authentic voice, and girls struggle with that. It's changing, but historically, there has been very little encouragement or support for that. So, that book has been an inspiration and a source of encouragement for so many girls, myself included."

AMY PASCAL

"My name is Amy Beth—*Little Women* has been with me my whole life. My father read the book to my mother when she was pregnant, and that's how they named me. I have a sister who is my best friend in the world. I understand how important family is and what it's like to have a sister that witnesses your childhood who's the person you can be the closest to."

ROBIN SWICORD

"I read the novel when I was eight for the first time. I read it every year of my life until I was about twenty years old. I read it in third grade after a steady diet of Nancy Drew and Hardy Boys and fantasy books. When I picked up *Little Women*, I felt that I was being confronted with the truth about family life. That siblings argue with each other. They do violence with each other. Parents sometimes abandon us when they feel overwhelmed. Often there's not enough money for important things—that was true in my family, and also that people we love die. That was my first exposure to a book that really respected the young reader. I felt respected by Louisa May Alcott. And I had a sense as a reader for the first time of not being able to understand everything in the book, which made me return to the book year after year until I got it all."

CHAPTER THREE

GOOD STRONG WORDS

✳

"Girls have to go out into the world and make up their own minds about things."

—MARMEE MARCH

Jo March, as played by Saoirse Ronan, awaits publisher Mr. Dashwood's response

Mr. Dashwood, as played by Tracy Letts, reads over Jo's manuscript

WRITERS HAVE AN EAR FOR language in the same way composers have an ear for the rhythms of sound. As Greta Gerwig wrote the *Little Women* script, she realized that there was no better source for the words to tell Alcott's story than the author herself. So, Gerwig returned to the novel time and again to find dialogue for her characters, in addition to using comments and observations taken from Alcott's letters to and from her loved ones. "I tried to use as much actual language from the book as possible," Gerwig says. "Every line in the movie is either from the book or from a letter or a journal. I wanted everything to be grounded in something I could point to."

Hearing the words spoken aloud, Gerwig was struck by how contemporary the speech sounded. "I had always had this idea of the cacophony of when they were young, how loud it was with four girls in one house," she says. "I wanted that very tight talking over each other to sound like a musical without music in a way. They're so famous, some of these lines. They're like Shakespeare in terms of being lodged in common memory. Saying them fast and casual and one on top of the other took away the preciousness. It made it so it didn't feel like every line had been embroidered on a pillow."

Gerwig did diverge from the source material in one vitally important way: Alcott's novel proceeds chronologically, beginning with the girls in adolescence and moving forward into their adult years. Gerwig's screenplay does not. She wanted to emphasize the March sisters as young women in the world, with flashbacks to the past playing out in a way that would have the soft, hazy glow of memory. The approach allowed her to explore different aspects of the sisters' lives and the struggles they face in their later years.

"Every other version, the film versions, had very much dealt with them as little girls,

(Opposite) The March sisters put on a performance

and then it basically ends in adulthood," Gerwig says. "What I had found so fascinating about the book when I was reading it as an adult were the parts where they're dealing with adulthood. Meg has twins, and she's trapped in a cottage with these twins all day. She's losing her mind and then she spends too much money on credit that she doesn't have. Their matrimonial discord around that could have been written yesterday."

"I wanted to put more emphasis on them as young adults, and make what was magical about their childhood feel almost bittersweet and achy because it's somehow gone," she says. "I wanted to give these characters a path to adulthood and keep what was special and unique and sort of irrepressible about who they were as children."

The story now opens with Jo in New York in the fall of 1868, setting aside her nerves and

Meg March hugs her twins, Daisy and Demi

boldly striding into a publisher's office to sell some of her fiction. Across the ocean in Paris, her youngest sister, Amy, is painting a staged scene of two gentlemen and a lady at a picnic along with a few other artists. Beth is back home in Concord, alone at her piano, playing to an empty room. Nearby, in her own modest cottage, Meg is struggling to make cranberry jam, sobbing in frustration at her failures, though the sudden appearance of her twins lifts her mood.

Although the film is rooted in the adult lives of the March women, Gerwig's screenplay retains all the best-loved episodes from their younger years: the sisters staging theatrical performances in the attic; artist Amy casting her foot in plaster and finding herself stuck in a bucket; Amy drawing an unflattering caricature of her schoolteacher in exchange for pickled limes; Jo accidentally searing off bits of Meg's hair as she helps her get ready for the New Year's Eve party at the home of the Gardiner family.

In a moment of artistic experimentation,
Amy's foot gets stuck in plaster

*Amy March, as played by Florence Pugh,
burns Jo's novel*

The painful moments are there, too: Jo cropping her locks and selling them to raise money for her father's medical treatment;

Amy burning the pages of Jo's novels in a fit of anger and jealousy; the family's immeasurable sorrow as they watch Beth grapple with the illness that will claim her life; the trauma and heartbreak when Jo tells Laurie she will never agree to be his wife.

Throughout, Gerwig was struck by the hardships that Alcott faced and how she nevertheless managed to create a fictionalized family that felt so perfect in so many ways. "I found the tension between the content of the book and the content of Louisa May Alcott's life really interesting," Gerwig says. "That break between what was, in many ways, a very unhappy childhood, then turning that into something that's seen as an idyllic childhood is, for me, fascinating as someone who writes. It's also heartbreaking. She has a quote: 'I have had lots of troubles, so I write jolly tales,' which just about makes me want to cry. She had a lot of sadness, but through that misfortune, she knew how to describe this idyllic childhood."

*Florence Pugh's Amy March, Eliza Scanlen's Beth March, and Jayne Houdyshell's Hannah
comfort Jo after she cuts off her hair*

Saoirse Ronan's Jo March brings the
family performance to life

CHAPTER FOUR

THE WOMEN (AND MEN) OF *LITTLE WOMEN*

✳

"We've got Father and Mother and each other."

—BETH MARCH

The crew films Friedrich's visit to the March house, as everyone sits down to dinner

JO MARCH

PORTRAYED BY

SAOIRSE RONAN

✳

THERE IS ONLY ONE JO MARCH. THE HEADSTRONG HEROINE OF *LITTLE WOMEN* was a character miles ahead of her time—a fierce and fiercely loyal young woman who prized her independence, her passion for writing, and her beloved family above all else. She can be gruff and disagreeable, quick-tempered and obstinate, but she is always clever and creative, resourceful and brave. No wonder generations of fans have fallen in love with her.

"She lives and dies by her family—they are her whole world," says actor Saoirse Ronan. "When she's with them, she's feisty and she's confident and she's outgoing. When she's with people that she doesn't know as well, she's a little bit more reserved. It's definitely her writing and the sisters around her that bring out this inner fire that she has inside of her."

Ronan has a history with fiery characters unafraid to go their own way. She earned a supporting actress Oscar nomination for her breakout role as a thirteen-year-old fledgling writer in *Atonement*, the 2007 adaptation of the acclaimed Ian McEwan novel. She's worked almost constantly ever since, starring in such films as director Peter Jackson's 2009 adaptation of the bestselling novel *The Lovely Bones*.

She earned her second Oscar nomination for her lead performance in *Brooklyn*, a film about a young Irish woman who finds love in 1950s New York, and her third for her standout turn in Greta Gerwig's *Lady Bird*, playing a teen in Sacramento, California, longing to

(Opposite) Saoirse Ronan's Jo March sits at her writing desk

break free from her family and find her own way in the world.

Reuniting with the writer-director for *Little Women*, Ronan enjoyed an important shorthand with Gerwig that helped the star relax into the demanding role. "It's been so great working with Greta again," Ronan says. "She's had a very clear overall picture of what she wants this movie to be and what she wants to say with it, but within that, she's allowed us to find it ourselves and do what feels right.

(Opposite) Jo March, as played by Saoirse Ronan, runs down the streets of New York after selling her manuscript

herself in her writing. That's where she finds her confidence."

She's far less clear-eyed about matters of the heart, which ultimately leads to conflict with Chalamet's Laurie, who adores Jo to her core. "Jo's got a very complicated relationship with love and romance," Ronan says. "For her, falling in love with someone automatically means

"I'm going to take fate by the throat and shake a living out of her!"

She wants every moment, every line reading, every movement that we give to feel like it's the right thing for us and it's the right thing for our version of this character."

And who is Ronan's Jo? "She is out-and-out a writer," says the actor. "She writes day and night. That's her whole life. That's how she makes sense of the world, and she's good at it. It's something that's hers, something that she always carries with her. She comes out of

that you have to marry them, which means that you give up any autonomy that you have. That's something that she never wants to do. So, she's essentially got this Peter Pan mentality where she wants to stay in childhood forever, and she wants her sisters and Laurie to feel the same, and they don't. They have this natural progression into adulthood that Jo is terrified of in a way."

Although romance proves elusive for Jo and Laurie, there's no question the two characters are soul mates, two halves of an entirely unique coin. Finding their relationship on set was easy for Ronan thanks to her rapport with Chalamet.

"There's a level of security that you can get from working with the same actor more than once," she says. "That brotherly, sisterly relationship that Jo and Laurie need to have, Timmy and I kind of have that anyway. I think you can see it with actors on-screen when they're physically very comfortable with each other. We're able to be ourselves around each other, and I'm able to hit him whenever I want because I know him."

Laura Dern, Saoirse Ronan, Florence Pugh, and Greta Gerwig share a laugh while filming Meg's wedding

"I don't like to doze by the fire. I like adventures, and I'm going to find some."

KEY PROPS

JO'S JOURNAL

Jo is frequently seen with her leather journal, which was handcrafted for the film by Devon Eastland, owner of the Larksfoot Bindery in Princeton, Massachusetts. To determine the right weight and color for every sheet of paper, as well as every pen and pencil the Marches and the other characters use, prop master David Gulick extensively researched writing in the Victorian era. "There are no fountain pens yet, so everybody's using dip pens," he says. "And nobody's using feathers anymore. It's really just ink and paper and pencil. Paper's still being manufactured, but it's not like the paper we have now. The writing paper would have been thin. The thinner it is, the more you can make out of the smallest amount of material."

JO'S SUITCASES

The vintage luggage was rented from the Hand Prop Room in Los Angeles, the only prop house in the United States with luggage dating back to the 1800s. Jo is seen with her bags when she travels by train from her Concord home to New York, where she takes a job teaching young children and hopes to make it as a writer. "Jo's fit her style," says Gulick. "We did screen tests with what she would be carrying so it didn't look like it was too few things." The prop master points out, though, that a lady of Jo's standing never would have carried her own suitcases in the 1860s. "If you were going to New York in a buggy and got on the train, then somebody would have delivered your luggage to wherever you were going," he says. "But Jo's not that person, so we had to give her something that she could carry."

(Above) Jo's handcrafted leather journal
(Right and opposite) Jo's travel luggage

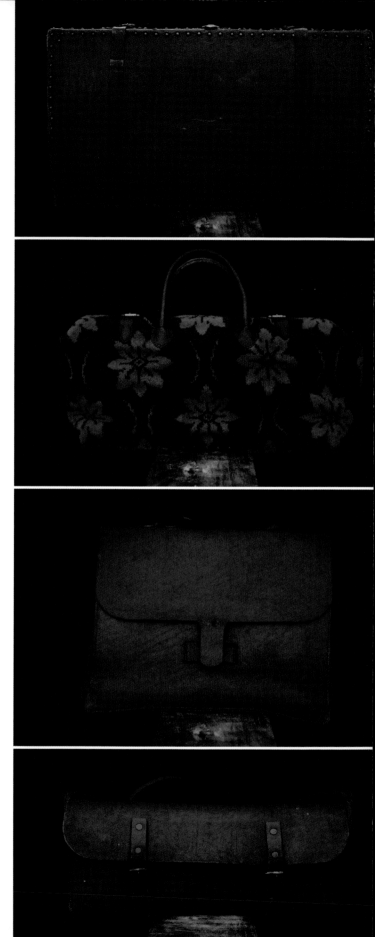

WET PLATE PHOTOGRAPHY

Also known as the collodion process, wet plate photography was invented and developed in the mid-to-late nineteenth century. The method is coming back into vogue as a unique, historical, and artistic way to take portraits.

First the photographer prepares a chemically-coated glass plate by dipping it in silver nitrate, then loads the plate into the camera. The photo imprinting requires a very high level of light and takes several seconds. Unlike more modern types of photography, wet plate photography has an incredibly short window to develop the photos. The photographer has to develop the photo with pyrogallic acid almost immediately—for this reason wet plate photographers work with mobile dark rooms.

These portraits of the cast of *Little Women* were taken on set, in between takes. All of the main cast got their portraits done as their schedules allowed and were able to see the development process as the on-set photographer worked.

The end results are historically accurate black-and-white photos, capturing the feel of the Civil War–era setting.

(Above) Stills photographer Wilson Webb develops the wet plate photographs, treating them with special chemicals to create a weathered look (Opposite) The wet plate photograph of Saoirse Ronan's Jo March

MEG MARCH

PORTRAYED BY
EMMA WATSON

※

EMMA WATSON IS TELLING SOME TRUTHS. "SISTERHOOD, IT'S NOT ALL HAIR-braiding and midnight feasts and solidarity," says the actor. "Sisterhood's brutal, let's be honest. But to me, that is how you become great, when you have people that surround you that challenge you, and I think the March sisters do that for each other."

As Meg March, Watson plays the oldest of the four siblings. At sixteen, she works as a governess to earn money for the family, but she remembers what life was like before the March clan fell on hard times. Often, in spite of herself, she pines for some of the niceties that other girls her age enjoy and for what her life might have been. "Of the four sisters, Meg is the more traditionally feminine," Watson says. "She's a romantic at heart in a way that Jo rejects. She's Jo's foil in that sense."

Although Watson hadn't read Louisa May Alcott's novel when she signed up for the role (it might be an American classic, but it is not taught as widely in the actor's native England), she understood the responsibility that came with portraying one of the much-admired sisters. "It was abundantly clear to me that this was a sacred text," says Watson, who launched her own book club, Our Shared Shelf, in 2016. "It was clear that this was a very important piece of writing and about a very important idea. I wanted to serve the story in any way that I could."

Research was a pleasure. "There's so much to inhabit with this part," Watson says. "I could read *Little Women* and then I could read an autobiography about Abigail, who was Louisa's mother, and I could read another one of Louisa May Alcott's books, *Moods*. I could read Emerson and Thoreau. The story is so rich that you can completely lose yourself in it. I'm not having to make much up or pull much out of thin air. There's so much detail and nuance there already."

Watson, of course, began her career bringing a very different but similarly beloved literary heroine to the screen, starring as

(Opposite) Meg March, as played by Emma Watson, reads a letter in the March family kitchen

brilliant bookworm Hermione Granger in the blockbuster films of the Harry Potter franchise. Since then, she's taken on a diverse array of roles in independent and Hollywood productions, including *The Perks of Being a Wallflower*, *The Bling Ring*, *Noah*, and Disney's live-action retelling of the animated favorite *Beauty and the Beast*, in which Watson starred as Belle.

Throughout her career, Watson has made it a point to play fully dimensional characters, and she has been famously outspoken

> ### "People don't have fortunes left them in that style nowadays, men have to work and women marry for money. It's a dreadfully unjust world."

on women's issues (in 2015, she delivered a speech at the United Nations discussing gender equality). When it came to Meg, Watson felt that it was important to acknowledge that while the character's desires for a husband and children are conventional, they are no less valid than those of her free-spirited sister Jo.

"Often there's this idea of what a feminist is, and to be a feminist you need to reject marriage and reject anything feminine," Watson says. "Meg's choice is a feminist choice. She wants to be a mother. She wants to be a wife. It's what she wants in her heart."

She finds her romantic match in tutor John Brooke (James Norton), who long harbors a torch for the oldest March girl with-

out her ever realizing his feelings for her. He goes so far as to purloin one of her gloves as a keepsake.

"I don't think Meg imagines herself ending up with someone like Mr. Brooke," Watson says. "She wants to fall in love, she wants to find someone kind, but she knows that her family is on the edge of destitution, and there is this pressure to find someone that can provide for her and her family in a very real way. Mr. Brooke arrives and he's not on her radar. As the story goes on, Mr. Brooke continually steps into the breach when there is need, when there is a crisis. He does the jobs that are unglamorous and difficult and that require patience, and he earns her love and her respect."

Although Meg and John do marry, she learns that there's no such thing as a fairy-tale ending. The way Greta Gerwig's script insightfully explores the myth of the easy happily ever after struck a real chord with Watson. The film sees Meg struggle with her new responsibilities as a wife and eventually as a young mother to boy-girl twins, Demi and Daisy, something the actor felt is rarely depicted on-screen.

"We're so used to seeing women get married, and then that's the end of the story," Watson says. "Seeing Meg try to navigate womanhood as a mother, as a wife, is refreshing. How do you juggle those roles? How do you protect and love and nourish a relationship when there's pressures and stresses on your relationship? When I read Greta's draft and I saw there had been this very careful tackling of these complex issues for women, I knew when I read the lines that saying them would be meaningful."

(Opposite, top) Daisy, played by Ava and Sophia Gelmini, and Demi, played by Brooks and Clark Moller, share a giggle on set (Opposite, bottom) Greta Gerwig goes over a scene with James Norton and Emma Watson

THEATER PROPS

Jo loves writing, Amy loves drawing and painting, Beth loves music, and Meg loves to act. Although she never seriously aspires to a career on the stage (despite Jo's urgings), the eldest March sister does take great joy in the homespun productions she stages with her siblings. The props department made the sisters' swords and shields, devising simple items from paint and papier-mâché. "You have to think, what would they have in the 1860s?" Gulick says. "How much money did they have and what could they afford?"

MEG'S SILK

In a Concord shop on a winter afternoon, Meg finds herself browsing with Sallie Moffat (described in the script as "a rich young woman who possesses an air of casual boredom that comes from never having to work for what you have" and played by actor Hadley Robinson). Soon after, Meg leaves with twenty yards of material she knows she can't afford. Wracked with guilt, she hides the bolt of fabric in a closet until she can think of a way to tell her husband about the ill-advised expenditure. "That was purchased from a big fabric house," Gulick says. "They still make silk in much the same way as they did in the 1860s. So, we just had to get the color right. We started with gray—it was scripted as gray—but I think we went with blue in the end."

MEG'S GLOVES

When John Brooke surreptitiously takes one of Meg's gloves, it's the first signal that he's terribly taken with the lady herself. But in truth, all the March sisters were meant to have pairs of gloves as part of their costumes in keeping with Victorian style. "We thought that the rules of wearing gloves and things would be more strictly observed in the costumes than they actually were," says costume designer Jacqueline Durran. "It turned out that what everyone wanted was a looser interpretation of Victorian that wasn't quite so rule bound. We prepared light-colored gloves that were handmade and handstitched, but in the end, we used a dark leather pair of gloves, unlined leather, very tightly fitted. They're not the modern type of gloves that have a cashmere lining or a fur lining. They're much more fitted leather gloves. Otherwise, they don't make the hand look as neat as it could."

(Top left) The homemade props and costumes for the March sisters' performances (Middle left) Meg's precious purchase (Bottom left) Emma Watson's Meg March eyes an expensive length of silk while shopping with Sallie Moffat (Opposite) The wet plate photograph of Emma Watson's Meg March

BETH MARCH

PORTRAYED BY
ELIZA SCANLEN

※

IT'S NOT EASY TO BE AN INTROVERT IN AN EXTROVERTED WORLD, BUT INSIDE THE March home, the boisterous sisters make a special place for sister Beth. "We live in a world where being gregarious and loud and exciting and amiable, that's what we aspire to be," says actor Eliza Scanlen. "Beth has this quiet energy about her, which I can really relate to. Marmee helps Beth to nurture this quiet power about her and to find strength in her shyness and to put value in being gentle. Nowadays I don't think it's something that we appreciate a lot."

Shy and retiring, Beth doesn't display the same grand ambitions as Meg, Jo, and Amy, but Scanlen argues that that doesn't necessarily make her any less interesting. The Australian actor sought to give Beth a rich interior life and a maturity brought on by illness. She's a character who understands her own mortality and the fleeting nature of life itself. "Beth is sick for a very long time," Scanlen says. "During that time, she goes through a journey of self-realization and discovery and a deep appreciation for childhood and how it shaped who she became, how it instilled in her certain values and a certain perspective on life. She's a very complex character."

Complex, yes, but also a world away from the dangerous, duplicitous character who brought Scanlen her first taste of real acclaim. She enjoyed a breakthrough role with her powerful turn as Amma, preteen half-sister to Amy Adams' troubled journalist Camille, in HBO's *Sharp Objects*, an adaptation of *Gone*

(Opposite) Beth March, as played by Eliza Scanlen, plays the piano at home

Girl author Gillian Flynn's dark mystery. Critics hailed her performance as a girl driven by violence and rage who turns out to be harboring horrible secrets that could destroy her small Missouri town.

It was a meaty role that harnessed Scanlen's innate talent, but it's fair to say the actor feels more of a connection to the retiring March girl. "Coming back to Beth has been a discovery for me, to be able to find strength in deep thought and kindness, which is something that we don't have enough of in the world," Scanlen says.

The Sydney native became interested in acting after attending the theater with her mother and her twin sister, and at an early

bonding between Beth and Laurie's grandfather, Mr. Laurence, who allows her to come to his house to play the piano that once belonged to his late daughter.

"Beth's passion for music allowed her to push past her shyness and was also a way for her to unify, even in times of crisis, the most important part of her life, her family," says Scanlen. "In many ways, Beth approaches life and love with simplicity, but music most definitely colored her world for the better and gave her confidence growing up alongside her three sisters."

Alcott's younger sister Elizabeth (known as Lizzie) served as the model for Beth, and like her literary counterpart, she died

"I know I'll get my music some time, if I'm good."

age, she began staging her own productions (not unlike Louisa May Alcott and her sisters), drafting her friends to participate. By the time she was in high school, Scanlen had landed a role on the soap opera *Home and Away*, which also helped launch the careers of Naomi Watts and Chris Hemsworth, among others.

For Beth, Scanlen not only dug deep into the March girl's psyche, but she also returned to an instrument she played as a child. The actor had studied piano for years when she stepped away from it in her teens. To prepare for *Little Women*, she began to practice again, playing two or three hours each day and learning new songs. Just as Jo has her writing and Amy has her painting, Beth expresses herself through her music— the piano serves as an important outlet for her. The instrument also becomes a point of

young, at twenty-two, from scarlet fever. Yet she found immortality in the pages of Alcott's novel. Her kindness and humility gave Beth two of her most important traits, and through the character, Lizzie continues to remind us that those who move through life quietly are no less significant than their boisterous counterparts.

"Strength can be found in different places and expressed in different ways," Scanlen says. "Strength can be found in vulnerability, too, and opening yourself up to feelings that you might not want to feel. Hopefully this film will be a way for people to appreciate introverts as people who have something to say and who navigate the world in their own way that's not less important."

(Opposite) The wet plate photograph of Eliza Scanlen's Beth March

Eliza Scanlen's Beth March plays the
Laurences' beautiful piano

KEY PROPS

BETH'S PIANO

Shy Beth finds her creative outlet in music—the piano becomes her passion. In the Orchard House set, the production made sure to include an accurate reproduction of the instrument played by Louisa May Alcott's sister Lizzie, who served as the inspiration for Beth; the color of both the piano cabinet and the upholstered green velvet bench are identical to the pieces that can still be found in the Orchard House Museum in Concord, Massachusetts today. Technically, though, the instrument isn't a piano, but rather an American melodeon, which is a type of nineteenth-century reed organ. In the Laurence home, however, Beth has access to a far more stately grand piano.

BETH'S DOLL

Beth's prized possession, Joanna, was a vintage doll with a porcelain face and hands that dates to the 1800s, Gulick says. "We made some other stuffed animals, but Beth's doll was purchased. There are a lot of dolls still around from that period." The prop master presented Gerwig with around twenty dolls, and she chose the one she felt Beth would hold most dear.

(Top right) The piano in the Laurence house (Center right) The piano Mr. Laurence generously gives to Beth (Bottom right) Eliza Scanlen's Beth March with her treasured doll (Above) A close-up of porcelain Joanna

KEY PROPS

MEDICINE BOTTLES

After visiting the destitute Hummel family and contracting scarlet fever, Beth is subjected to a raft of ineffective treatments before dying far too young. "The medical part was interesting, because really all medicine was killing people," Gulick says. "When someone would get sick, they'd give them mercury, they'd give them lead, they'd give them arsenic to kill the disease. They bled people. They had very little anesthetic. The French were just developing clean operating rooms. There was plenty of morphine to go around, but other than that, there was not much in the way of keeping things clean and using the right instruments."

It was important to Greta Gerwig that her film more realistically depict what Beth would have endured than earlier movie versions had, given that losing her has such a profound impact on Marmee and the other March sisters. "Greta did not want to make it clean and easy," Gulick says. "She wanted to make it sad and uncomfortable." In addition to the bleeding apparatus that was used by doctors at the time, Gulick procured an array of powders, liquids, and tinctures to scatter around Beth's bedroom. None contained any of the dangerous substances; they were filled instead with slightly more palatable potables. "One was cream and a little instant coffee to darken the cream," Gulick says.

(Above and right) An array of treatments, tinctures, and medical supplies cover Beth's bedside table

"We can't be afraid of death any more
than we are afraid of life."

AMY MARCH

PORTRAYED BY
FLORENCE PUGH

⁎

BRIGHT AND BEAUTIFUL AND SUPREMELY CONFIDENT IN HER OWN GIFTS, Amy March is the youngest of the sisters, and, according to actor Florence Pugh, the most misunderstood.

"Everybody's perception of Amy is that she's the sour one in the family who is spoiled and has everything and gets what she wants," says Pugh. "What I loved about this is that you get to see her brilliance and her sensitive side, how complicated and human she is. She's mischievous, she's cheeky, she fantasizes about romance and love and money and riches. She's an artist, and she's incredibly passionate about being the best version of herself as an artist or she won't do it at all. She's quite a feisty character to play."

It's perhaps the ideal role for a twenty-three-year-old English actor whom the *Guardian* newspaper once described as "formidable." After making her screen debut in 2014's *The Falling*, Pugh captivated critics in 2016's thrilling indie *Lady Macbeth*, in which she played a seventeen-year-old sold into marriage in the 1800s who finds surprising ways to claim her own power. She played Cordelia opposite Anthony Hopkins in 2018's *King Lear* and had a lead role in the six-part John le Carré adaptation *The Little Drummer Girl*. Additionally, she starred opposite Chris Pine in *Outlaw King* and in *Midsommar*, director Ari Aster's follow-up to the horror hit *Hereditary*.

(Opposite) Amy March, as played by Florence Pugh, in the school room

Amy sketches in the gardens of a Parisian estate

what it is to be a sister. They love each other. They hate each other. They talk over the top of one another. They kiss each other. They cry for each other."

Despite the March's modest circumstances, Amy aspires to a life of luxury where she can dedicate herself to art. (In real life, Alcott's youngest sister, Abigail, also known as May, was a talented painter who studied in Boston and Europe; in 1877, one of her works was displayed at the Salon in Paris.) She's vocal about what she wants from life and determined to better herself and her station.

"The book was important to me because it didn't just highlight these four very angelic girls," Pugh says. "It also talked about their hunger, how passionate they are to achieve and how passionate they are to want to make something of themselves. That's always attractive to read, whether it's about women or men."

For Pugh, acting is in the family blood. Like Amy March, she has three siblings (Pugh is the second youngest), two of whom are also actors. Her older brother, Toby Sebastian, played Trystane Martell on *Game of Thrones*. Her older sister, Arabella Gibbins, is a stage actor. The close-knit relationship between Pugh and her siblings gave her plenty to draw from when sketching out how she wanted to approach playing Amy, and it was the aspect that she found most relatable in Louisa May Alcott's novel.

"The sisterly bond is everything," Pugh says. "That's the whole book. It highlights

On-screen, Amy and Jo's stormy personalities bring them into conflict—namely, after Amy, in a fit of jealousy and anger, burns the only copy of Jo's novel. But working together on the film, Jo actor Saoirse Ronan was impressed with the gumption Pugh brought to the youngest March girl. "She has done something with Amy that I don't think anyone else has ever done before," Ronan says. "She's given her this bite. She's not a girly girl. She's got this fire to her that only an actor like Florence could bring to that role."

(Opposite) The wet plate photograph of Florence Pugh's Amy March

"Talent isn't genius, and no amount of energy can make it so. I want to be great or nothing."

"I have ever so many wishes, but the pet one is to be an artist, and go to Rome, and do fine pictures, and be the best artist in the whole world."

KEY PROPS

AMY'S ARTWORK

Amy is a prolific artist even in her youth—the bedroom she shares with Beth is covered with pencil sketches and other artistic flourishes (including a white lily painted on the wall). When she later travels to Paris to study, she produces oil paintings in the same realistic style as the eighteenth- and nineteenth-century artists she most admires. To create her paintings, the production turned to artist Kelly Carmody, based in Waltham, Massachusetts. But Florence Pugh appeared to be a natural on-screen, making the art feel very much her own. "She looks accomplished when Amy is drawing or painting," says prop master David Gulick. "She's practiced."

AMY'S WOODEN BUCKET

In one of the more comedic episodes from the March sisters' youth, Amy attempts to make a cast of her foot and finds herself stuck in the bucket of plaster. Gulick found a simple wooden bucket from the time for the scene. "Plaster of Paris was pretty common," he says. "You would have greased your foot up and put it into the plaster, poured it around. It would have gotten really hot, and you could easily get stuck. Your foot is tapered, so you can get it out if you put some kind of lanolin on your foot and move it around, and the plaster isn't too high."

(Above) Amy's paint palette (Left) Amy's sketches decorate her and Beth's shared bedroom in the March house

ANATOMY OF A SCENE
AMY FALLS THROUGH THE ICE

It's one of the most harrowing moments in *Little Women*. Amy, desperate to make amends with Jo after burning her sister's manuscript in a fit of jealousy, follows Jo and Laurie out to the pond near their home where the friends plan to go ice skating. Still furious with her sister, Jo ignores her while she and Laurie race along together farther and farther away. Then, Jo hears a splintering crash and a scream that stops her heart cold. The youngest March girl has plunged through the surface of the ice and is on the verge of drowning in the freezing waters below.

Determining the best way to stage the dramatic moment wasn't easy. One option was simply to film the sequence on a stage surrounded by green screen and add digital imagery after the fact to match the natural pond environment at the Concord location. But according to visual effects supervisor Brian Drewes, that approach simply wouldn't have been in keeping with the grounded, real-world approach of the rest of the film.

"It didn't feel like the right solution for this kind of filmmaking," says Drewes, whose company Zero VFX handled the roughly two hundred visual effects shots in the film. "The March house is up there at the location. The Laurence house is up there. It's all geographically tied in, so there's a lot of feeling when you're there. Often, when you put somebody on a green screen set, you end up losing a little legitimacy with how they feel and that ends up on the screen—even if technically it may be easier to solve it that way. You may not end up with the performance that you want."

Instead, the production opted for a practical approach that would be augmented later using digital imagery. The special effects department, led by special effects coordinator Andy Weder, installed a system of piers that hugged the edge of the pond at the location where the exteriors of the March and Laurence homes stood. Drewes spent a great deal of time at the site mapping the area so it could later be re-created.

"Probably three days before the scene was shot, we went out there and did a very precise survey of the entire property of the Laurence house, the March house, and the pond area," he says. "For that we used a system called LIDAR, which is basically radar. We go all the way around the perimeter of the pond to capture the geometry of the landscape, because we're going to re-create that all digitally. We're going to have a digital re-creation of the pond area and also the whole estate, so then, as we're relandscaping it, we know what was there."

Although the special effects department initially considered installing an artificial skating surface on top of the piers, that turned out to be not only cost-prohibitive but

Crew members, Saoirse Ronan, and Timothée Chalamet prepare to shoot the scene

also unfeasible for the VFX team. They would not have been able to convincingly disguise the flat surface to make it appear to be real ice. "The problem is that it's white," Weder says. "It doesn't have any reflectiveness to it. That's what they want, the CG guys, that's what they like to see. When the lake is frozen, there's a little reflection there."

"It's not a modern-day skating pond," adds Drewes. "It hasn't been groomed. It's got some natural aspects to it. Reflections is one of the main things that we ended up seeing."

Instead, a reflective plastic surface known as Lexan was put in place to act as the surface of the ice, but the Lexan couldn't be nailed in place due to the extreme winter weather. "When the sun hits it, it expands and it shrinks, so we did have an issue when the wind picked up and pulled a couple of pieces off and almost threw it in the water," Weder says. (The solution? Heavy-duty, clear packing tape.)

Director Greta Gerwig reviews the camera footage with crew members

At one end of the covered pier, the crew installed a tank of water that measured 8 by 8 by 4 feet and was covered with a clear acrylic surface, which was then waxed: That was the tank of water that Amy actor Florence Pugh would later fall into when the youngest March sister tumbles through the ice. "The floating wax looks like floating ice," Weder says. "It gives you a little glare and it kicks off a little shininess from the sun."

Special skates were required to help the actors and their stunt doubles glide across the faux ice. Prop master David Gulick found skates from the period made from brown leather and steel, which the special effects department then copied and modified. They used two different sets of roller bearings coated with polyurethane that could be inside the prop blades. "From a distance, you can't tell if it's ice skates or if it's roller blades because they're smaller wheels, so it's not like roller blades where you glide a lot," Weder says.

In the morning, when the surface was most like ice, harder wheels were preferable, but as the surfaced warmed and became less slippery, the softer wheels provided more traction. "The stunt people who were using them discovered that whatever foot they push off from, they liked the traction one, and the foot they glide on, they like the other ones," Weder says. "So, they would combine the wheels."

Six pairs of skates were built—one pair for each stunt person, and one pair for Saoirse Ronan, Timothée Chalamet, and Florence Pugh. Joe Grossman, an ice-skating instructor and coach for the Harvard women's hockey team, gave the actors lessons

The special skates designed for the faux ice

with the specially made skates and was on set during the filming of the sequence.

Pugh (and her stuntwoman) bore the brunt of the discomfort when filming the scene on a cold December day in Boston. When Amy falls into the ice, Pugh was plunged into the water tank rigged beneath the pier. And though that water was warmer than the actual lake, it was hardly warm enough to be comfortable, hovering between 55 and 62 degrees. "The fight we had with the water is the temperature," Weder says. "Since it's so cold outside, if I bring that up to a certain temperature, it steams, and we can't have steam."

To keep them warm during filming, both Pugh and her stuntwoman (who sometimes had to remain in the chilly tank for fifteen-minute stretches) wore wet suits beneath their costumes. Between shots, the women retreated to an industrial fish tank that was heated to 100 degrees and acted as a makeshift Jacuzzi. "We're in the Northeast," Weder says. "That's what you gotta get."

After filming had wrapped, Drewes' job began in earnest. He and the other artists at Zero VFX took the footage shot at the location and set about integrating the piers and the artificial surface seamlessly into the natural environment surrounding it, making sure the light bounced off the ice just as it would in nature. "The pond is a naturally occurring pond, and the platform sort of rings around the edge of it," Drewes says. "What we ended up doing is raising the water level of the real pond to match the decking that is much higher off the water. We're essentially filling this pond with another foot or two of water and freezing it over digitally. The end result will look like they're on ice."

Florence Pugh, as Amy March, sits in the water in between takes (Following spread) Cinematographer Yorick Le Saux films Laurie and Jo pulling Amy out of the ice

MARMEE
MARCH

PORTRAYED BY
LAURA DERN

❋

LAURA DERN READ *LITTLE WOMEN* WHEN SHE WAS THIRTEEN YEARS OLD, AND THE novel felt like a revolutionary discovery. "I remember deeply Marmee's advice to Jo about honoring your own anger," says the Oscar-nominated actor. "That stayed with me. I had read so many stories that were about shutting out things that weren't pretty or appropriate, and Louisa May Alcott wrote about the mess and allowing yourself to be a full human being. And a maternal character advising that? That was radical for me in the eighties, you know? It's a message that children still need to hear. Be your true, deep self and don't let anybody talk you out of your sass, your anger, your vulnerability, your sensuality, your humor, your grace. That's who you are."

Casting Dern as Marmee seemed an obvious choice—she's a singular talent who has made it her life's mission to portray a range of multifaceted female characters on-screen. Most recently, she earned an Emmy for her supporting role as a working mother in the Bay Area in the prestige miniseries *Big Little Lies*, and she was nominated for her turn as a documentary filmmaker grappling with a difficult childhood in the heartrending drama *The Tale*.

"Portraying strong female characters in any movie is something I really care about," Dern says. "In this film, 'strong' is defined in many different ways, and that's what's so special about *Little Women*. Louisa May Alcott established strength as ambition, strength as independence, strength as art, strength as marriage and parenting, strength as being an activist."

(Opposite) Laura Dern as Marmee, the beloved mother of the March sisters

Laura Dern's Marmee prays over Beth as her sickness worsens

"The love, respect, and confidence of my children was the sweetest reward I could receive for my efforts to be the woman I would have them copy."

As Alcott did with the other characters in her groundbreaking novel, she rooted Marmee's passion for caring for others in the traits of her own mother, Abigail, who Dern extensively researched before coming to set. "Her mother was an abolitionist, a feminist, America's first social worker," Dern says. "She was an incredible woman. She was that kind of mother that would respect you as an equal and not speak down to you as the child. I think that carries the heart of the whole piece and is the reason why Louisa had the boldness to become the writer she was, being raised in that kind of energy."

On set, the actors playing the sisters gravitated toward Dern in the same way that Louisa May Alcott and her siblings were drawn to Marmee. "She's incredibly maternal and warm," says Saoirse Ronan. "She's a wonderful mother herself, and that radiates from her. She's managed to make Marmee very much her own woman. There's private moments where she's at a breaking point and she's about to fall apart, but she pulls it together and puts a smile on her face for her girls. Laura has such incredible skill as an actor that she's able to show that in a couple of seconds on-screen."

*(Opposite) The wet plate photograph of
Laura Dern's Marmee*

AUNT MARCH

PORTRAYED BY
MERYL STREEP

✳

"No one is paying you to think."

EVERY FAMILY HAS AN AUNT March—the older, opinionated grande dame of a relation who has a fondness for naps and no qualms about making her point of view known, frequently at the most inopportune occasion. To portray the uproariously blunt relative, who lives at the posh Plumfield estate with her chatty parrot, *Little Women* sought out the grandest dame of them all, Meryl Streep. The universally lauded acting legend brought gravitas to the character as well as humor, even a touch of whimsy. "Meryl is hysterical as Aunt March, hysterical," says Emma Watson. "Everyone knows someone that is just that person that is so unfiltered to the point of hilarity. That's what Aunt March is, and that's what Meryl does brilliantly."

(Opposite) Meryl Streep in costume as Aunt March (Above) Aunt March's treasured poodle

"You can be right and foolish."

Florence Pugh, Meryl Streep, and
Greta Gerwig share a smile on set

THEODORE 'LAURIE' LAURENCE

PORTRAYED BY
TIMOTHÉE CHALAMET

❊

BEFORE MOST READERS ARE INTRODUCED TO THE TRIFECTA OF BROODING AND remote nineteenth-century literary heartthrobs—*Wuthering Heights*' Heathcliff, *Jane Eyre*'s Mr. Rochester, and *Pride and Prejudice*'s Mr. Darcy—they typically encounter Theodore "Laurie" Laurence. Brooding and remote (naturally), Laurie is an orphan who has only his tutor, John Brooke, and his stern grandfather, Mr. Laurence, for company in the sprawling estate that sits across from the March sisters' modest home.

Then Jo March enters his life.

"Laurie is Jo's best friend," says actor Timothée Chalamet. "He's friends with all the girls. He doesn't have the most idyllic childhood perhaps. Financial holdings he does, but he's not privy to any sort of social behavior because he has no friends, and he's homeschooled and he's locked up with Mr. Brooke, essentially. He finds unique and amazing and tantalizing and root-like relationships with these girls that help him grow, particularly in Jo, who he falls in love with."

Chalamet's upbringing couldn't have been more different. He grew up in a family passionate about the arts (his sister Pauline also acts professionally), attending Fiorello H. LaGuardia High School of Music & Art and Performing Arts before studying at Columbia University and New York University. He made his feature film debut in 2014 in *Men, Women & Children*, directed by Jason Reitman, and appeared in Christopher Nolan's *Interstellar* the same year. Roles in several indie productions followed.

(Opposite) Timothée Chalamet's Laurie after telling Amy not to marry Fred Vaughn

Jo and Laurie's fateful first encounter at the Gardiner's New Year's Eve party

In 2017, Chalamet graduated to A-list status with performances in both Greta Gerwig's *Lady Bird*—as Kyle, the, well, brooding and remote teen who steals Lady Bird's heart—and in *Call Me by Your Name*. His sensitive turn as seventeen-year-old Elio, who falls for his father's assistant, played by Armie Hammer, in 1980s Italy, earned him a best actor Oscar nomination. On the heels of that success, he starred in 2018's *Beautiful Boy* as a young man trapped in the painful cycle of addiction, recovery, and relapse.

The opportunity to reunite with Gerwig and to again work with *Lady Bird* star Saoirse Ronan made it easy to sign on to *Little Women*. "Saoirse's one of my favorite people I've ever worked with," he says. "I feel like I'm often learning from her. I appreciate the fact that her energies, her talent as an actor, the way she accesses her talent, is so palpable. It's an amazing thing to be around. She's just so good."

Although Laurie develops a special bond with all the March girls, it's obvious from the start that he and Jo are mischievous soul mates, impish wits with a distaste for rules, inventive minds entirely content to go their own way in life. Their interplay certainly suggests that they're meant to be together, but, sometimes, life has other plans.

The scene in which Laurie professes his feelings to Jo and suggests they marry only to be rebuffed by her remains one of the most painful in classic literature—and it's no less heartbreaking watching Ronan and Chalamet live out the exchange on-screen.

"Laurie and Jo are like two sides of the same coin," Chalamet says. "They complete each other in a way, certainly in their youth. There's a case to be made for the fact that their best friendship would lead into a great married life, which is a big theme and source of contention. Because of that best friendship, the exact opposite argument can equally be made that they would tear each other apart."

(Opposite) The wet plate photograph of Timothée Chalamet's Laurie

77

Jo and Laurie, both heartbroken after Laurie's confession, discuss their relationship

KEY PROPS

MAILBOX KEYS

As part of a plan to clandestinely communicate with the March sisters—and to thank them for admitting him into their secret attic society—Laurie installs a post office in the hedge for the passing of letters, manuscripts, books, and bundles. He presents each sister with her own key, tied with a different color of ribbon. "I bought keys that looked good and then we aged them down," says prop master David Gulick. "They were brass, so you just had to hold them in your hands to give them the appearance of looking worn. You use sandpaper and a little bit of muriatic acid to knock it down a little more. Hydrochloric acid watered down is basically muriatic acid. It's what you use on brick walkways to clear them up."

LAURIE'S RING

The ring that Laurie wears was a gift from his beloved Jo. The piece was designed by London jeweler Jessica de Lotz, who makes jewelry with authentic nineteenth-century stamps that were purchased at auction. Costume designer Jacqueline Durran selected a ring from the line bearing an image of a steam train with the word "Quick" engraved at the top. "I felt that it should be something that looks like a quirky, individual, unique sort of piece," Durran says. "It's like a piece of jewelry that would be exchanged between two young people, almost children. It's what they have and what they have to give. It's not overly precious."

(Above) A brass key to the secret attic society's post office box (Opposite) Saoirse Ronan's Jo March checks the sisters' secret post office box

FRIEDRICH BHAER

PORTRAYED BY

LOUIS GARREL

❋

IT TAKES A TRULY SPECIAL MAN TO WIN THE HEART OF JOSEPHINE MARCH. Friedrich Bhaer is a poor philosophy professor who has emigrated to New York to find a better future and earn money to help educate his two orphaned nephews. He meets Jo early on in her days in the city—they live in the same boardinghouse and share a passion for literature, theater, and progressive ideals. He's far less fond, however, of the sensationalist tales Jo sells to make a living.

"He's from a world that she desires, the world of books and intellectuals," says French actor Louis Garrel who plays Jo's romantic match. "He is a teacher. He is from Europe, and I think she can dream about the world he comes from. Sometimes when two people meet, suddenly something happens. There is no explanation. It's a passionate and very deep relationship between them."

When *Little Women* was published, fans were outraged that their beloved heroine jilted Laurie in favor of a man nearly twenty years her senior who is described as having bushy hair and lacking "a really handsome feature in his face." (Greta Gerwig arguably deviated from Louisa May Alcott's vision by hiring Garrel, once voted one of France's sexiest men.) He also has no qualms about harshly critiquing Jo's work, urging her to put her talent to better use. But Ronan says that Garrel's approach to

the character brought out all the qualities that Jo finds so magnetic and so admirable. "He's managed to bring this humility to Friedrich, to take lines that could be so harsh and cold and make them very honest. You do fall in love with that honesty that Friedrich gives to her. No one's ever pulled her down a peg or two, and I think she's needed that."

Still, Garrel, son of respected French filmmaker Philippe Garrel and actor Brigitte Sy, says he sometimes felt out of his depth working with Ronan in their most explosive scene. "The first time that I had to act with Saoirse, I felt that she was the first violin of the orchestra, and I was like an inferior violinist trying to follow her," he says. "She's got a very particular speed when she plays. She's very quick. And I'm not quick. My English is not so fluent. She was so quick that sometimes I was a bit afraid to be too slow."

(Opposite) The wet plate photograph of Louis Garrel's Friedrich Bhaer

COLLECTED WORKS OF WILLIAM SHAKESPEARE

Friedrich presents Jo with a beautiful token of his esteem after he spies her standing near the back of a performance of *Twelfth Night* (the vintage edition of the Bard's works was purchased from a London retailer). The handwritten note that accompanies the gift reads as follows:

For the writer in the attic:

Because you enjoyed the play so much tonight, I wanted you to have this. It will help you study character and paint it with your pen. I would love to read what you're writing, if you'll trust me. I promise honesty and whatever intelligence I can muster,

Yours, Friedrich

"I feel to know the strong-minded lady who goes so bravely under many horse noses, and so fast through much mud."

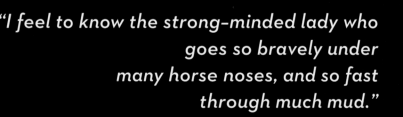

(Left) Friedrich Bhaer brings his gift to Jo at the boarding house

JOHN BROOKE

PORTRAYED BY

JAMES NORTON

❋

JOHN BROOKE CERTAINLY ISN'T AS SHOWY AS HIS TEMPESTUOUS STUDENT LAURIE, but he's solid and dependable. Admirable, even. "On the page, John's referred to as being a bit stiff and boring—you know, that trope of a tutor being a little bit conservative," says actor James Norton. "We decided that that was a bit predictable, so we played with that. He's a little bit gauche, I guess."

Meet the new John Brooke, who is still solid, sweet-natured, and dependable, but he's perhaps got a more robust sense of humor and maybe more on his mind. "He's very much involved in the Transcendentalist movement and is quite a spiritual and serious guy and a deep romantic, it turns out," Norton says. "He's a sweet individual who's probably not particularly experienced with women. A bit like Laurie and many men those days, when women arrive in his life, he's baffled, intrigued, and a bit overwhelmed by the whole situation. It's probably not that dissimilar to my own experience when I was a young man."

Norton himself was interested in serious things as a young man—attending Catholic school and studying theology before enrolling at the Royal Academy of Dramatic Art in London. He appeared in prestigious theatrical productions, including *The Lion in Winter*, and went on to film and television roles, playing a violent psychopath in *Happy Valley* and an amiable vicar who solves mysteries in the series *Grantchester*.

On the *Little Women* set, his costars found Norton charming and his take on Laurie's lovestruck tutor a delight. "James Norton has played John Brooke beautifully," says Saoirse Ronan. "He's given him so much heart, and he's made him really funny, which I don't think anyone was expecting. And he's just gorgeous."

(Opposite) The wet plate photograph of James Norton's John Brooke

"I won't trouble you. I only want to know if you care for me a little, Meg. I love you so much, dear."

FATHER MARCH

PORTRAYED BY

BOB ODENKIRK

⁜

IF LOUISA MAY ALCOTT WAS A WOMAN AHEAD OF HER TIME, THE SAME COULD certainly be said of her parents, Bronson and Abigail, both of whom shared radical notions about the role women should play both in society and in the home. "Bronson believed that women and girls should be educated and that they should become whatever they want to be," says actor Bob Odenkirk. "He was a fighter for education for women and for minorities—in the 1880s! He was a very thoughtful person, a very forward-thinking person, a very enlightened person."

Odenkirk plays the March family patriarch, a character based on Bronson (though, in reality, it was Louisa, not her father, who left the family for an extended time to serve in the Civil War, not as a minister but as a nurse). "So many of the qualities of the father are true qualities of Bronson Alcott," says Odenkirk, an Emmy-nominated actor well known for his starring role on the drama *Better Call Saul*. "Like many intellectuals, he was on fire with new ways of looking at the world and inventions. He's a little bit lost in his head. He somehow seems disconnected from the world around him because he's living in his head so much."

(Opposite) The wet plate photograph of Bob Odenkirk's Father March

"Rather a rough road for you to travel, my little pilgrims, especially the latter part of it. But you have got on bravely, and I think the burdens are in a fair way to tumble off very soon."

Bob Odenkirk's Father March bids Jo farewell at the train station as she moves to New York.

HANNAH

PORTRAYED BY
JAYNE HOUDYSHELL

※

HANNAH MIGHT NOT OFFICIALLY BE A MEMBER OF THE MARCH FAMILY, BUT THE love shared between the housekeeper, the sisters, and Marmee is boundless and unconditional. "She's an important source of support and love for both Marmee and the March girls," says actor Jayne Houdyshell. "She's seen them through their lives. She's more than a stereotypical loyal housekeeper. She has a very active part in raising the girls."

Houdyshell is an award-winning actor with a resume that goes back decades and features dozens of acclaimed turns on the New York stage in addition to roles in film and TV. Her relationship with Louisa May Alcott's novel dates to her childhood—she first read *Little Women* when she was nearly ten years old and felt an immediate connection to the book. "I grew up in a family of four girls and no brothers, so to be introduced to this extraordinary family of sisters was very exciting for me as a child," she says. "I love the way she depicts the relationships with the sisters because the bond is great and the love is very strong, but there's nothing idealized or saccharine about that."

When she lost one of her sisters at the age of twelve, Houdyshell sought solace in the pages of *Little Women*. "We had been four and then three, and the challenge of that kind of loss to a family is a very particular kind of thing. It's so beautifully and poignantly portrayed in the book *Little Women* when Beth passes away. Ultimately what triumphs always in this family and throughout this book is the love they have for one another, especially in times of adversity and loss and difficulty and challenge."

Playing Hannah on-screen, Houdyshell made her a constant, watchful presence. "She wants what's best for the girls, certainly," the actor says. "She hopes for all of the girls, as was traditional during that time in history, that they all find the right mate and have happy married lives and healthy, strong families."

(Opposite) The wet plate photograph of Jayne Houdyshell's Hannah

"Now, my dear young ladies, remember what your ma said, and don't fret. Come and have a cup of coffee all round, and then let's fall to work and be a credit to the family."

Amy and Beth kiss their beloved Hannah

MR. LAURENCE

PORTRAYED BY
CHRIS COOPER

※

"I had a little girl once, with eyes like these."

A MAN OF FEW WORDS BUT MUCH PRESENCE, MR. LAURENCE IS GRANDFATHER TO wayward Laurie. But beneath his stillness lies a great deal of emotion and grief for his two lost children: his son, Laurie's father, and a young daughter gone far too soon. To portray Mr. Laurence, the filmmakers cast Oscar-winning actor Chris Cooper, a veteran of stage and screen known for his performances in *American Beauty* (1999), *Adaptation* (2002), and *August: Osage County* (2013), as well as for his work on Broadway.

Cooper lent the distinguished gentleman a certain stillness and remove that melts away as his abiding fondness for Beth March comes to the surface. "He has a gentle soul that is so palpable in Mr. Laurence," says Beth actor Eliza Scanlen. "Chris has a very calming nature about him. That's something that both of our characters have, this quiet power. Mr. Laurence's power is more intimidating—Beth is warmer and more inviting—but somehow these two opposites are able to unite in this understanding of perhaps feeling a bit insecure and feeling a bit self-conscious about their quietude."

(Opposite) The wet plate photograph of Chris Cooper's Mr. Laurence

KEY PROP

MR. LAURENCE'S SLIPPERS

To thank her affluent neighbor for his generosity—first, in allowing Beth to visit his home to play piano and, later, for gifting her one of her own—Beth fashions for him a regal-looking pair of deep violet slippers adorned with detailed embroidery. "The slippers are a close interpretation of the description of them in the book," Durran says. "We tried to get the flowers the same, and they're described as purple in the book."

"The piano suffers for want of use. Wouldn't some of your girls like to run over, and practice on it now and then, just to keep it in tune, you know, ma'am?"

(Above) The embroidered slippers that Beth creates as a thank-you gift for Mr. Laurence (Left) Mr. Laurence, as played by Chris Cooper, during a breakfast scene

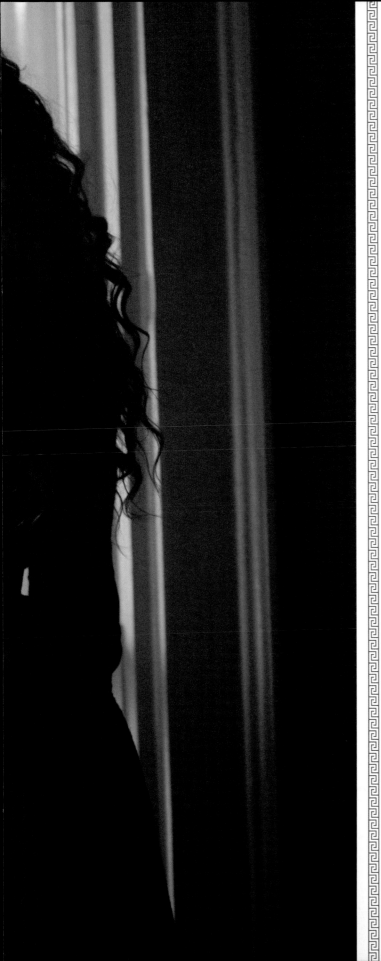

CHAPTER FIVE

DESIGNING WOMEN—

CREATING THE COSTUMES

✳

"I don't believe fine young ladies enjoy themselves a bit more than we do."

—JO MARCH

A crew member makes adjustments to Jo's Christmas dress

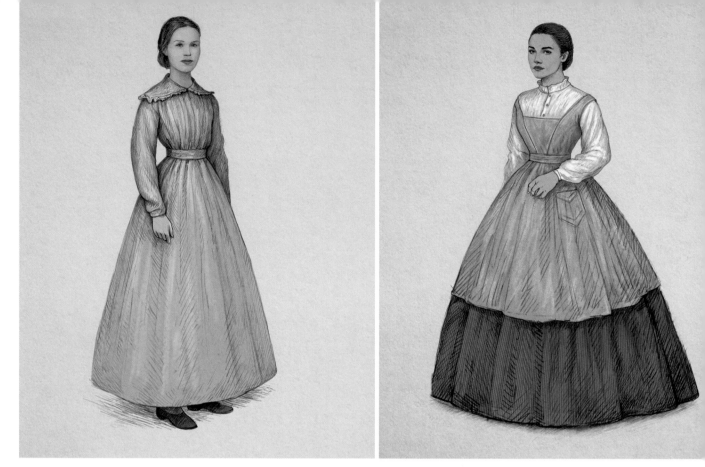

AN EARLY LOOK

FASHION MAGAZINES MIGHT FEEL like a relatively modern invention, but the most iconic, *Vogue*, launched in 1892. It wasn't the first. France's *La Mode Illustrée* was popular throughout the second half of the nineteenth century, while in America, women often turned to two periodicals, *Godey's Lady's Book* (1830–1898) and *Peterson's Magazine* (1842–1898).

When Oscar-winning costume designer Jacqueline Durran began designing looks for *Little Women*, she consulted all four.

"We tried to take shapes and styles from the exact magazines of the period, which the March girls would have had, and then slightly interpret them to fit our other brief, which is to make it accessible," Durran says. "It was about finding ways of representing the Victorian world as real people and not making the period costume something that distanced you from what was going on in the drama."

If anyone can make Victorian clothing accessible to a modern audience, it's Durran. The London-based costume designer has an extensive background in period costume dramas. She won her Academy Award for 2012's *Anna Karenina*, and she designed lived-in looks for 2005's *Pride & Prejudice*.

Drawing from Louisa May Alcott's novel and Greta Gerwig's screenplay, she designed costumes for the lead actors that would visually underscore attributes of each of their personalities. "There's Jo in the way we know her as someone who would rather be a boy," Durran says. "Meg's look evolved into some-

thing that had a quite fairy-tale aspect, a love of things medieval. Beth, she's the most passive. She doesn't particularly make any strong statement in how she dresses. Amy is the dressed-up one. The key thing was to make a look where each girl had her specific character and at the same time you could pull them together as a family."

The time-jumps in the movie that take the Marches from 1861 to 1869 also played a role in how Durran conceptualized the key

(Above) Putting the final touches on Amy's dress at the New Year's ball (Opposite) Concept illustrations for several costuming options

costumes. "Each person has a different look depending on what time period they're in," she says. "Amy has the most dramatic change, because she goes from being a dressed-up child to being a very dressed-up adult. Jo has a more subtle change because she's not clothes-obsessed. Her look evolves, but it's not so radical. Amy's is the most radical. Meg changes. She's less fantasy and more motherly. The detailing on her costumes changes more than anything."

Dressmaking supplies at the fabric
and tailoring shop in Concord

Frida Aradottir, department head of hair, secures Meg's beachside hat

MEG MARCH

ROMANTIC AND MATERNAL

Playing up the fairy-tale aspect of the eldest March sister's costumes involved adding bits of whimsical detailing like tiny rosettes and crocheted lace. (Notably, Durran had created actual fairy-tale costumes for Emma Watson for her starring turn as Belle in *Beauty and the Beast*, including the voluminous yellow gown she wears in the closing ballroom scene.) It was a notion that Durran and Watson developed together.

"There's a way of finding characters through what you put on as an actor in the morning, and so many of my ideas about Meg were centered around her love for the natural world," Watson says. "She has all this jewelry that's flowers and brooches to reflect that. Of the four sisters, Meg is probably the most elegant dresser, even though she doesn't have much money. She doesn't do tons of frills and ribbons, but everything she wears is very carefully cut and tailored and considered and feminine and elegant. She has this homemade elegance."

The gown she wears for her wedding to John Brooke carries forward those ideas, emphasizing the slightly fairy-tale theme.

"It's made of silk, it's got vintage lace, it's very simple, very pretty," says Durran.

Throughout the film, the garments in Meg's wardrobe hew to the overall color scheme Durran created for the sisters' wardrobe. Jo's colors are red and blue; Meg's are green and lavender. Beth is usually dressed in shades of pink or mauve, while Amy has a fondness for pale blue. "It's complimentary in that it's the same sort of tone of girliness," Durran says. "The thing about those colors that is important is that it doesn't become schematic. You have to take it as a guideline and interpret it rather than following it [to the letter]."

The one real exception is the dress Meg wears to the Moffat's springtime ball. Sallie Moffat loans her a gown since the one Meg had brought to wear to the party is too modest and out of fashion. The pink dress with the unforgiving bodice and delicate sleeves fit Watson like a (missing) glove, but it was very much not in keeping with Meg's usual style. "The Moffat's is the pastel ball," Durran says. "It's as beautiful as America gets. It's ten or fifteen girls in shades of pastel in a beautiful pastel room. It's a very obvious and easy-on-the-eyes idea of beauty or prettiness."

Meg, wearing her borrowed pink dress, runs into Laurie at the Moffat's springtime ball

Meg seeks a moment of privacy at the
Moffat's springtime ball

JO MARCH

SPIRITED AND UNCONVENTIONAL

It's only fitting that Saoirse Ronan's tomboy should, in fact, wear boy's clothes. But not just any boy—specifically, her boy Teddy, as she's fond of calling Laurie. "They swap waistcoats," Durran says. "They wear things of each other's. The plan was that they would have things that were interchangeable between the two of them because they were such close friends and they identified with each other. It's a nice way of expressing their relationship."

"I wanted them to be androgynous halves of the same whole," adds Gerwig. "He quite literally is a boy with a girl's name, and she's a girl with a boy's name. They're flipped sides. They are not mates. They are twins in that way. They're often dressed exactly the same."

Although Jo's wardrobe still falls within the Victorian period, her garments have a strong masculine influence. Ronan suggested to Durran—who first met the actor on her breakthrough film *Atonement*—that the jacket Jo wears when penning tales in the attic have a soldierlike feel. "It was Saoirse's idea to have a military jacket as her writing costume," Durran says. "We reinterpreted military so that it felt more fantasy."

Like her sisters, Jo is usually dressed in cotton, linen, or wool and is often seen wearing a knitted sontag. A Victorian triangular shawl also known as a bosom friend, the garment crosses in front of the body and ties in the back. The design kept a woman's torso warm and

Jo in her military-inspired writing costume

Saoirse Ronan in one of Jo's waist coats

her arms free of extra layers. The pattern first appeared in *Godey's Lady's Book* in January 1860.

The March girls also have colored petticoats, which was quite common for the time. (Jo's favorite is red, a nod to her fiery inner nature.) But the outspoken sister studiously avoids the most constraining item in a Victorian lady's wardrobe. "This part we cheated slightly because not everyone wears a corset," confesses Durran. "Amy has to wear a corset in Europe. Meg wears a corset when she's grown up. Jo never wears a corset. If you were really doing a Victorian costume, you'd have a chemise

at the bottom and then your corset over the top of your chemise. Then, if you have a hoop, you'd have your hoop, and then your petticoat, your bloomers. Then you have your skirt, then you have your blouse and your jacket."

Naturally, hoops aren't anything Jo is interested in wearing, either. "Jo was at one point going to be wearing a hoop for her costume in New York, but she doesn't wear one anymore," Durran says. "It was again trying to increase the informality of Victorian clothes and suggest the Bohemian world that these girls were in where they didn't conform to those fashions."

The March sisters visit the beach

BETH MARCH

FEMININE AND ROMANTIC

Beth's costumes have a softness to them that mirrors her gentle demeanor. "There's a certain playfulness that is a big part of her costuming," says Eliza Scanlen. "She usually wears warm and inviting colors. I worked with Jacqueline on creating this makeshift, slipshod quality to her costumes. She might be missing a button or her collar might not come around all the way or she might not be wearing her buttons all the way up. There's a certain forgetfulness about her."

For the sequence when Beth and Jo go to the beach—the determined older sister positive that the fresh ocean air will restore her ailing sibling to health—Durran had the opportunity to create a summer look for the characters that was quite different than the heavier fall and winter apparel they most often wear. "It's not feasible that they would have had those clothes in their wardrobe, but it needed to be a kind of expression of the perfect summer's day, so they had to be dressed differently for it," Durran says.

Of course, Jo's efforts to heal her sister come to naught, and when Beth dies, the sisters go into mourning. The mourning costumes, again, were tailored to suit each of the principal characters. "There are extremely extensive rules on mourning for Victorians," Durran says. "There's a whole stratification, and each stage is marked out very specifically. The mother would have been in the deepest mourning. The sisters would have been in deep mourning but less. But more than anything, we went with what felt right for the person. Laura Dern

was in a dress that was very similar to her best dress, but it's black. Meg has a dress that's the same sort of style as one of her best dresses. Hers is gray rather than full black because it was one stage less."

Jo's mourning costume was dark gray and had a flecked texture. "Jo wouldn't necessarily be the sort of person who, once Beth had died, would have a new costume to wear straight away, so we introduced elements of Jo's mourning costume before Beth had died," Durran says. "Before Beth dies, Jo is already wearing her mourning skirt. It seemed to work that she would be going into mourning step-by-step."

Determined to keep the memory of her beloved sister alive, Jo begins to wear Beth's jacket, which was made from handwoven wool—except for the cuffs, which were made from scraps of fabric left over from a dressing gown belonging to the late Oscar-winning actor, Sir Alec Guinness. "Jo wears it because it was Beth's; that's what she would do," Durran says. "There's a sort of overlap in styles among the girls. It was intended that the cutoff between their own individual costumes be quite loose. They wear different pieces of each other's things. Even though you want each girl to have her own style within the group, it's nice for those edges to blur a bit."

(Opposite) A green coat decorates Beth and Amy's room

The exterior of the millinery shop, named
after cinematographer Yorick Le Saux

Florence Pugh's Amy March with Emma Watson's Meg March

AMY MARCH

ELEGANT AND REFINED

The most fashionable March sister seems tailor-made for Europe, where she's gone with Aunt March to study painting when the film opens. "Amy, when she gets to Europe, she wears silk more than anything," Durran says. "She always wears a hoopskirt because [that's] what you should be wearing in 1868. The whole thing about Amy in Europe is much closer to 1868 fashion than the rest of the girls back in America. Europe was on a different level of chic. That's what Amy's costumes represent."

Amy is perhaps at her most elegant at the New Year's Eve soiree she attends in the City of Light, attired in an elaborate gown that Durran says is especially accurate to the period. "It's black satin, and it has an old gold, dark yellow trim. The skirt has a black silk tulle overskirt, and the yellow trim is also edged in black beading with a tail running down the back. It has quite a large hoop and quite a large skirt."

One of Durran's favorite pieces for Amy is a cape that makes only a brief appearance on-screen—she wears it once, when Laurie comes to visit her in her studio. It was made entirely from antique pieces. "The cape was a special garment," the costume designer says. "I, in my cupboard of things in my house, had embroidery pieces that were cut off of two beautiful shawls that had been eaten by moths. The embroidery was intact, so we used that old embroidery repositioned on cream-colored fabric to make her cape. The cream-colored fabric was a wool flannel that we bought that by coincidence was also vintage. I can't remember how many weeks it took to sew for, like, ten seconds of screen time."

(Opposite) Amy in the art studio, during a scene with Laurie

LAURIE

SINGULAR AND UNORTHODOX

Just like the March women, Laurie's wardrobe is split between his older and younger years. "He has a young look where he's like the quirky poetic outsider that never looks like anyone else," Durran says. "When he grows up, he starts wearing suits more. He has a sort of European chic but still with the slight strangeness of Laurie. He's not quite mainstream." One of the key references for his costumes was a painting by James Tissot from 1868 of a group of Parisian men. "Those men had the sort of detailing that Laurie would have because he was traveling in Europe, and he got his clothes in Europe," Durran says. (Laurie's clothes weren't the only ones to be inspired by fine art; one of Jo's blouses was based on a Winslow Homer painting, and the shirt she wears at the end of the film for scenes at the Plumfield estate was copied from a Renaissance painting.)

Laurie, as played by Timothée Chalamet

Laura Dern's Marmee watches over a sleeping Amy

MARMEE

BOLD AND BOHEMIAN

Durran wanted Marmee's progressive spirit to shine through in her wardrobe. "She has elements that are more straightforwardly Victorian, but she's a hippieish Marmee," Durran says. "She was keen to be in an unstructured, more relaxed home look when she's not doing something public." Durran incorporated the colors that the March girls wear into Dern's costumes and had some fabric specially printed for select garments. "She always likes to have an element of bright color to contrast with anything dark she wears."

CHAPTER SIX

HOME IS WHERE THE HEART IS

✳

*"I've got the key to my
castle in the air, but whether
I can unlock the door
remains to be seen."*

—JO MARCH

(Opposite) The March sisters let Laurie, played by
Timothée Chalamet, into their secret society

The exterior of the March family home

THE CITY OF BOSTON WAS FOUNDED in 1630, and as one of the oldest metropolitan areas in America, it exudes a rare historic charm. It's difficult to find a street or a corner of the city that wasn't the site of some memorable event from centuries past. Remarkably, Greta Gerwig's *Little Women* was the first adaptation to shoot entirely on location in the greater Boston area and in Concord, Massachusetts, where the Alcott family home Orchard House still stands today.

The production headed to the city and its environs hoping to capture the spirit of the place Alcott called home. "It has an intangible benefit, something you can feel," Gerwig says. "What was magical about it was that we were largely based out of Concord, and you can go to see Louisa May Alcott's house! She literally lived right down the street from

Ralph Waldo Emerson. Then you can walk twenty minutes to Walden Pond, where Thoreau wrote the greatest Transcendentalist works. Down the street the other way, you have the North Bridge where the first shots of the Revolutionary War were fired. Being there and shooting on that land added something very meaningful."

Gerwig also opted to shoot *Little Women* on film, as opposed to using digital cameras. In her mind, the classic approach was the perfect fit for a story of such weight and scope. "I think we chronically underestimate and place less importance on women's stories, especially stories of domesticity, stories that happened away from the battlefield," Gerwig says. "If you were to make an epic that took place over ten to twelve years about a bunch of men in the Civil War, you would shoot on film. You would have the most beautiful locations. It would be epic. It would be sprawling. It would be made

---

(Opposite) The Concord street set

The March's living room, decorated for Christmas

to look important. I wanted this to have that epic scope and let it be huge even though it is domestic. I wanted it to be big. I wanted to shoot the movie like it matters."

All in all, the production visited roughly thirty-eight key locations—nine of which had never hosted a film shoot before. "We are shooting in places where the Alcotts were when they were growing up," says supervising location manager Doug Dresser. "They would have walked through these forests. They would have walked down these streets. They crossed those bridges. It's breathing the same air. It's watching the same sunrise. It's looking at the same trees."

No setting was as important as the March residence, the unassuming structure that func-

tions as the emotional center of the movie. It's the place where the March sisters are most at ease and where so many of the pivotal moments in their lives occur. "It's the anchor of the film," says production designer Jess Gonchor. "Their house is the house where there's always a fire lit, and it's always warm and cozy and everybody wants to go. It's like when you're growing up, it's the house that every kid wants to hang out at."

Gerwig and Gonchor wanted the exterior of the March house to sit in relatively close physical proximity to the Laurence house (the interiors of the March residence were constructed on the Franklin, Massachusetts, soundstages that served as the headquarters for the production). Neither was interested

INSIDE ORCHARD HOUSE

Few historic sites exude warmth and vibrancy in the same way as Orchard House, the landmark residence where Louisa May Alcott lived and wrote *Little Women*. Originally constructed in the 1600s, the two-story wooden structure is not only a remarkable artifact from America's colonial days but also a time capsule from the 1800s, when its most famous occupants transformed the home into a center of creative expression and progressive thought.

The Alcotts moved to Orchard House in 1857. When Bronson Alcott purchased the property, it was the two hundred acres of land and the accompanying apple orchard that seemed of the most value. The two dilapidated houses (which were later joined into one) were in terrible repair, and most assumed they would be torn down. Instead, Bronson spent nearly a year on renovations, crafting a residence that would be ideal for his wife and daughters.

On the ground floor of the home was the Alcott parlor, the kitchen, the dining room, and Bronson's study, where he would host literary luminaries from the era, such as Nathaniel Hawthorne, and close friends Henry David Thoreau and Ralph Waldo Emerson (the latter of whom would share books with young Louisa).

Upstairs were the bedrooms shared by Bronson and Abba, Anna and Louisa, and Lizzie and May, until Lizzie's death in 1858. Her beloved piano, given pride of place in the parlor, became a tribute to her memory. The parlor was also the place where Anna Alcott married John Pratt wearing a handmade dress with a simple lace collar.

Both the piano and the dress can be seen at Orchard House, which stands today looking much as it did in the Alcotts' time. Opened as a museum in 1912, the historic site contains many of the artifacts and personal effects that once belonged to Alcott's family, including the original brown knee boots Louisa May Alcott wore for her role as Rodrigo in the sisters' theatrical productions, as well as original furniture, drawings on the walls by May Alcott, and other paintings and portraits.

Orchard House is open to the public year-round and offers a range of educational activities, including guided tours, craft workshops, and "living history" programs that allow guests to interact with members of the Alcott family. Executive director Jan Turnquist, who served as a key behind-the-scenes advisor on *Little Women*, plays Louisa May Alcott herself and says that visitors have included former secretary of state Hillary Clinton and former first lady Laura Bush; photographer Annie Leibovitz included several images shot at the museum in her 2011 book *Pilgrimage*.

"This house has become an important place for people to have as sort of a touchstone," Turnquist says. "If they love the book—or even if they're just curious about this book that seems to get so much attention—they like to come here and see almost everything in the house as original items that were owned and used by the Alcott family. It feels like they just stepped out the door."

Director Greta Gerwig at the helm, as
Saoirse Ronan's Jo March stands watch
in Beth's sickroom

in relying on digital trickery for the landscape shots, so they needed to find a large open plot of land adjacent to an impressive estate.

"It was very important to Greta to have the houses face each other, to see the way they looked at each other," Dresser says. "You can tell the story of the relationship between Jo and Laurie or the March family and the Laurence family in one easy image. It says a lot about the relationship of the two families by the way the two houses look."

They found what they were looking for at a private residence in Concord that was originally built in 1938. The European-inspired five-bedroom home was situated on more than fourteen acres of land and surrounded by immaculate gardens and rolling lawns. Gonchor and his team built a slightly modified replica of the real Orchard House at the site.

It took nearly twelve weeks to construct the three-story March house and paint and landscape the exterior. "It definitely referenced the Alcott house, the real house," Gonchor says. "Our house is much bigger, but a lot of the geography and the flow and the circulation is the same—the siding on it, the painting on it, the simplicity of it. It was all painted one color. It's a dark-stained house that wanted to be one with the environment, like a mushroom growing in a field, as opposed to the Laurence house, which is the white knight shining and glistening in the sun."

"We wanted to have the outside of the March house feel like a beautiful old wooden jewelry box, so the outside is wood tone and brown," he adds. "When you open it up, it's an Easter egg. There's some beautiful velvet in there."

Throughout the first-floor rooms—the parlor, the dining room, the kitchen—there is a real sense of life in motion. It's easy to recognize the interior of the March home as a lively place where conversation and creativity can thrive and all are welcome. "The first floor is pretty colorful," Gonchor says. "As you go up

The March family living room

The March family home, decorated for Christmas

to the second floor, it's a little bit more personalized to the girls that are living there. Finally, the attic is dark but still with a lot of life and some vibrancy. It's like a gradient reversed from nature, which is dark at the bottom and lighter to the sky. This is very colorful on the first floor, and as you go up, it gets more into the reality of a lonely attic."

Of course, nowhere in the March home is truly lonely. The attic provides a quiet, solitary space for Jo to write, but it also hosts some of the sisters' impromptu theatrical performances and clandestine meetings and is littered with props and costumes, even a copy of their handmade newspaper, the *Pickwick Portfolio*. "There were no video games, no iPhones," Gonchor says. "This is how they occupied their time."

Set decorator Claire Kaufman adorned the attic space with items representing each sister. "Amy is this amazing artist, so instead of doing a lot of drapery, we painted a big drape across the back wall," Kaufman says. "The girls all hang out up there, so we wanted to get little

bits of each of them into that space, but it's a very raw wood space. We put in crafts that the girls would have made. We took these big natural tree branches and cut little things to hang off of them, flowers they would have dried and kept up there. I tried to do more flowers in the attic and to do more herbs and natural things that would be in the kitchen that they would use. There was sewing stuff up there for Meg, who loved to sew, and of course, there's Jo's whole writing niche. We tried to put some musical stuff up there for Beth as well."

The external walls of the March house set

(Opposite) Stand-ins help set up a scene in Beth and Amy's bedroom

The Laurence house, by contrast, has little evidence of joy in its corridors. To convey an overwhelming sense of solitude, the production traveled to a 1904 mansion in Lancaster, Massachusetts, that had the right kind of forlorn energy. "What we were looking for in the interior of the Laurence house was a bit more space, a little bit more separation, a little bit more loneliness," says Dresser. "We found a house that fit that almost in a *Citizen Kane* kind of way. It's darker in tone. The light is different. It's a little more formal."

"I don't want to say it was devoid of warmth, but we wanted the audience to get the idea that Laurie is jealous of the lifestyle and the closeness and the camaraderie going on inside the March house," Gonchor adds. "We wanted the audience to know he was wealthy but he was unhappy in there."

Kaufman chose large, ornate furniture for the home. "I found this very heavy dark Italian carved furniture, and we used a lot of dark greens and jewel tones for the drapery and the upholstery. We were lucky because we had these very large, grand rooms. You could think about scale and not have to put a lot in them, just important pieces to anchor the room and have these beautiful things in there. It makes it feel kind of lonely, whereas the March house, it was very eclectic, lots of interesting fabrics, lots of interesting textures, lots of color. You've got these four girls in this family all living in this house, so there's a lot more going on. There's a lot more stuff in there, a lot more layering."

The exterior of the Laurence Estate

Eliza Scanlen's Beth enters the Laurence Estate

Newspaper pages decorate the interior of the Weekly Volcano *set*

BOSTON PLAYS NEW YORK— AND PARIS

Early in the film, in a burst of joy, Jo runs through the streets of 1868 New York after selling her writing to the gruff Mr. Dashwood (*Lady Bird* actor Tracy Letts) at the offices of the *Weekly Volcano*. For the street scenes, the production transformed a small piece of Lawrence, Massachusetts, into the bustling big city.

The transformation took roughly six weeks to complete, but getting it right was critical given that the moment was such a pivotal one, according to set decorator Claire Kaufman. "We shot it for one day, but it's so important because it's basically the opening of the film," she says. "I want to make sure that people believe these characters are in these places because of the details, because of the way it looks."

Little Women also traveled to the boulevards and parlors of Paris without ever leaving the confines of New England. Many of the European sequences were filmed at the historic Crane Estate in Ipswich, Massachusetts. (The estate was also the location for the movie's beach sequences.) The 2,100 acre piece of land, named for Chicago industrialist Richard T. Crane, boasts spectacular scenery and three

(Opposite, top) Extras bring the New York City set to life (Opposite, bottom) Detailed set decorations create Little Women's *New York*

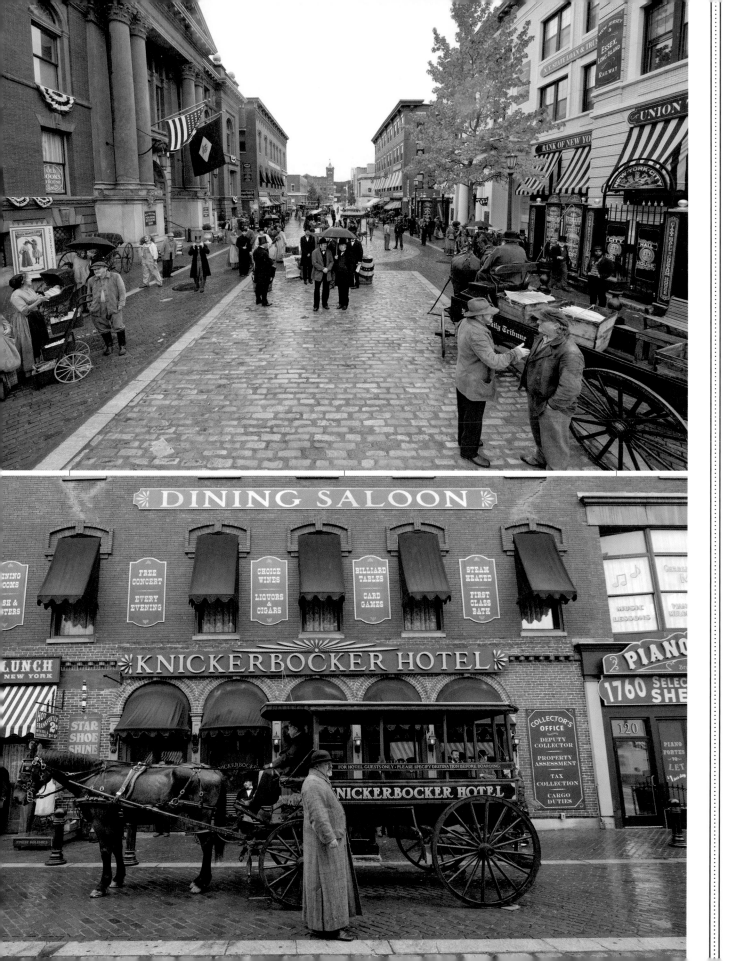

A frustrated Jo walks through the streets of New York after an argument with Friedrich Bhaer

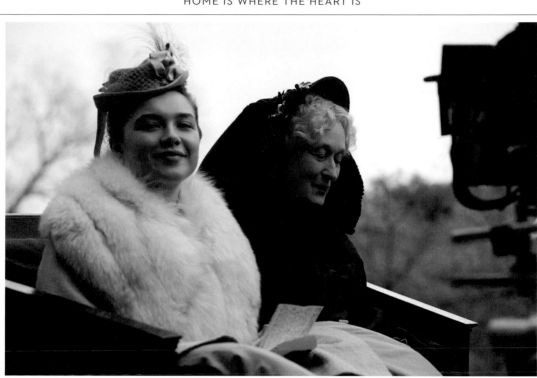

Florence Pugh and Meryl Streep prepare to film Amy and Aunt March's carriage ride through Paris

separate properties: Castle Hill, Crane Beach, and the Crane Wildlife Refuge.

Atop Castle Hill sits a fifty-nine-room Stuart-style mansion designed by David Adler and furnished with period antiques. "The gardens are rich and it's on the ocean and the scale of it is amazing," says production designer Jess Gonchor. "It was a unique place that would definitely pass for being in Europe."

For the all-important scene where Laurie and Amy reconnect in Paris on the afternoon of New Year's Eve 1868—the youngest March sister spies the jilted twenty-six-year-old while seated beside Aunt March in an open-air carriage—the production visited Arnold Arboretum of Harvard University. Founded in 1872 and named for whaling merchant James Arnold, who bequeathed

the land for the study of plants, the site had never hosted a film shoot. "Because it was *Little Women*, because there is a literary tradition of environmentalism and protection of the natural environment, they were willing to open the doors to us," says location manager Douglas Dresser.

The Arnold Arboretum offered precisely the right mix of beautiful mature trees and a wide promenade that evoked the feeling of a Paris city park from the mid-nineteenth century. With horse-drawn carriages and more than one hundred extras in period costume, it was like traveling back in time—except, perhaps, for the modern snacks. "We ate fries in the carriage," says Amy actor Florence Pugh brightly. "I was with Meryl Streep on a carriage eating chips. When does that happen?"

(Opposite, top) Set decorations inside Concord Station (Opposite, bottom) Crew members prepare to film a scene at the Concord Station set

CHAPTER SEVEN

LIVING LIKE THE MARCHES

✳

"I'd rather take coffee than compliments just now."

—JO MARCH

*Laura Dern's Marmee and Chris Cooper's
Mr. Laurence share a smile as they create Christmas
decorations for the March home*

Greta Gerwig directs the cast for a scene with Hannah, Beth, Amy, and Meg

THE MARCHES' EXTREME DO-IT-yourself approach extended to every facet of their lives, often out of necessity but sometimes out of sheer entrepreneurial spirit. "When they're in their home, it's quite a bohemian lifestyle that they have," says Saoirse Ronan. "They're very emotive. They're very creative, incredibly expressive, through themselves and their work and with the way they are with each other."

The March approach to Christmas was a perfect example of the artistic flair they brought to special occasions. With money difficult to come by, they turned to nature for holiday decor. "It was important to bring the outside in, even though it's winter," says set decorator Claire Kaufman. "What we tried to do for the March girls is drive home the fact that they were these really imaginative, creative girls that wanted to do so much with not a lot. For the Christmas sets, they can't go out and buy decorations, so it was researching what they would have and what would be accessible to them."

For Kaufman, that meant hanging pine garlands on the sets and using fruit and other edible treats to decorate their Christmas trees, one of which was trimmed with real candles. Living as they did in the days before electricity, the Marches relied on oil lamps and candles to illuminate their home as well as the centerpiece of their holiday decorations.

"We got a tree that was spindly, not a big full tree," Kaufman says. "It was important to me

(Above) A close-up look at the March family Christmas tree (Opposite) Emma Watson, Saoirse Ronan, Florence Pugh, and Eliza Scanlen as the beloved March sisters

to do that because that's what people did. No fake tree. It was going and cutting down a fresh tree and then putting candles on it and dried oranges and stringing popcorn. I tried to be true to that and what people did in that era."

Food stylist Christine Tobin also focused her efforts on creating dishes that were authentic to the Victorian era. "As simple as the food was back then, we were able to bring in color with the things that they would have in their backyard," Tobin says. "The March family, how they presented food was to take elements of the outdoors to adorn their cakes and platters. They didn't have the money to purchase pretty ribbons and things."

Three weeks before filming began, Tobin oversaw a massive undertaking to prepare as much food as possible for the shoot. She made dozens of jars of blueberry compote, raspberry, blackberry, and mixed berry jams, preserved plums, preserved pears, an array of pickles, and upwards of sixty pickled limes for the scenes when young Amy and her schoolmates are consumed with enthusiasm for the citrus treat. (The limes sound unusual, but they were, in

(Opposite, top) Supplies for homemade Christmas decorations in the March's living room (Opposite, bottom) Platters of pears, sweet potatoes, and sausages fill the table on Christmas morning

fact, wildly popular among children in the 1860s and were routinely sold in sweet shops, often for a penny each.)

Although Tobin researched historical recipes for the film, she says the farm-to-table approach that's wildly popular among chefs now was commonplace in the nineteenth century, and so she ultimately adopted a similar, less-is-more philosophy. "It's all simple cookery, roasting and blanching and usually locally sourced ingredients," Tobin says. "They had this garden and apple orchard, so they used what was in their backyard, the Alcotts. That's how people lived then."

As she was shopping for ingredients, Tobin sometimes would find items that she would bring back to help decorate the sets. "I would go to my local farms, and when I would see things that were about to go in compost, like a perfectly rotten pear, I would ask, 'Can I take all this?' It was to have things look like they'd been

The March family table on Christmas morning

sitting for a while. Not everything was perfect and looking mass-produced then. There's spots on things. But ugly food was made beautiful because it's placed and elevated in a space."

Wanting to draw a distinction between the Marches' and the Laurences' disparate economic circumstances, prop master David Gulick hit upon the idea to differentiate even the flour that was used in the baked goods in their respective homes. "We used white flour in the Laurence house and dark flour in the March house just to show a difference in wealth," he says. "You didn't bake with white flour if you were a regular family. There would not have been much white flour for making pastries in the March house or for cooking."

The exception, though, was the pastries. For those, Tobin turned to some of the finest bakeries in Boston to supplement the vast quanti-

ties of homemade treats she and her assistant, Boston chef Carolyn White, were turning out on a nearly daily basis.

"I used a lot of recipes, especially in the baked goods area, from modern cookbooks out of London," Tobin says. She was looking for recipes that stylistically were rooted in the past but modernized. "To research and recipe-test real old-world recipes would have taken forever," she says. "Their flour was so different. The baking then was heavy and eggy and dense. That's not very attractive. If you want to see this beautiful spread of tiered cakes, you have to balance that out."

One of the most important spreads of delicacies arrives at the March house on Christmas morning courtesy of their wealthy neighbors—a beautiful bounty of pastry, confectionery, and most stunning of all, copious

A beautiful cake from the Moffat's springtime ball

Food stylist Christine Tobin, assistant prop master Morgan Kling, and props assistant Grace Gulick touch up the Christmas feast

Christine Tobin makes final touches to the Marches' decadent Christmas feast

amounts of peppermint ice cream. The frozen delicacy is not something the March sisters would have been able to routinely enjoy. "To display a large amount of ice cream in the 1860s, first you had to have it made, then you had to keep it cold," Gulick says. "You couldn't do that then unless you spent a lot of time and money."

Tobin brought in three, twenty-five-gallon containers of vibrant, locally made ice cream for the scene. "The color had to be very specific, because it was scripted as being pink and the girls are in awe," Tobin says. To keep it cold, Gulick and Tobin placed the large scoops of the ice cream in a giant silver bowl that had been in a freezer, replacing anything that looked too melted with other scoops that were kept nearby on dry ice. "To have fake ice cream in such an important scene would not have worked," Tobin says. "It's OK if things were a little melted, because that's what would have happened at that time."

HOW TO MAKE DISHES LIKE THE MARCHES

✳

*"I'll learn plain cooking for my holiday
task, and the next dinner party I have
shall be a success."*

—JO MARCH

*The March family table, elaborately decorated for
the Christmas feast*

PEPPERMINT ICE CREAM

MAKES 1 QUART

This peppermint ice cream was scripted to be part of the pivotal food scene where the March girls come home to find the gift of an elaborate Christmas feast from the Lawrence family. Our director stressed the importance of the ice cream being pink.

The ice cream used for this scene was made by a Boston ice cream company, Puritan Ice Cream, that has been making ice cream for more than one hundred years. A perfect match for our nineteenth-century food scene.

The ice cream is indeed REAL. There were more than fifty scoops filling the punch bowl. We had to move quickly, and I had to replace melting scoops in between takes. Our actors were licking their fingers as the ice cream slowly dripped down the sides of bowl. We went through 75 gallons of ice cream for this scene.

People often marvel over the fact that I use only fresh, real food on film sets. "Can we really eat this?" is asked often. I love sharing beautiful foods with people and a film set should not be any different. There are many benefits to displaying time-sensitive foods on camera. Having the actors licking their fingers with joy is one of them! —Christine Tobin

¾ cup sugar	1 cup heavy cream
2 large eggs	2 teaspoons peppermint extract
1 Tablespoon cornstarch	6 drops red food coloring
2 cups half-and-half	¾ cup crushed peppermint candies

In a medium mixing bowl, beat the sugar into the eggs until thickened and pale yellow. Incorporate the cornstarch and set aside.

In a heavy medium sauce pan over medium heat, bring the half-and-half to a simmer. Remove the pan from the heat, and slowly beat the warm half-and-half into the egg-and-sugar mixture. Pour the entire mixture back into the pan and place over low heat. Stir constantly with a whisk or wooden spoon until the custard thickens slightly. Remove from the heat and pour the hot custard through a strainer into a clean, large bowl. Allow the custard to cool slightly, then stir in the heavy cream, peppermint extract, and food coloring.

Cover with plastic wrap and refrigerate until cold or overnight.

Stir the crushed peppermint candies into the chilled custard, then freeze in one or two batches in your ice cream maker, according to the manufacturer's instructions. When finished, the ice cream will be soft but edible. For a firmer ice cream, transfer to a freezer-safe container and freeze for two hours or more. Scoop and enjoy!

RASPBERRY HAND PIES

MAKES 16 HAND PIES

This treat was used as a staple in the March's baking repertoire. Filled with raspberry jam, these butter crust hand pies were a favorite of our Marmee. Like many of the treats designed for *Little Women,* these cookies are sprinkled with granulated sugar. —Christine Tobin

FOR THE DOUGH:

1 cup all-purpose flour

2 tsp granulated sugar

Salt

½ cup cold, unsalted butter, diced

¼ cup cold water

FOR THE HAND PIES:

Rasberry jam, for filling

Milk, for brushing surface of pies

Superfine sugar, for sprinkling

To make the dough: In a large bowl, combine the flour, sugar, and a pinch of salt. Add the diced butter. With your hands or a pastry cutter, mix the butter with flour and start breaking the butter into bits until you get a crumb-like texture. Mix in the cold water, 1 Tablespoon at a time, until the mixture comes together to form a dough. This dough should not be overworked. Flatten the dough ball with your hand and wrap in plastic wrap. Chill for at least two hours, but overnight is best.

To make the hand pies: Preheat the oven to 350°F. Roll out the dough until it is about ¼ inch thick. Using a 3 inch round cookie cutter or a drinking glass, cut out as many circles as you can. Place about 1 teaspoon of the raspberry jam in the middle of one dough circle, brush the edges with milk, and cover with another dough circle. Press the edges together gently with your fingers. To really seal the edges well, press the edges down with a fork. Brush the top of each hand pie with milk, and sprinkle with granulated sugar. Repeat until there are no remaining dough circles.

Place the hand pies on a cookie sheet, and bake for 20 to 25 minutes or until the bottoms are a nice golden brown.

PICKLED LIMES

MAKES 10 TO 12 LIMES

These pickled limes are made with a very simple recipe and patience. Sucking on these limes was an indulgent pleasure for young children in New England during the nineteenth century. —Christine Tobin

10 to 12 limes	**Large box kosher salt**

Rinse the limes and cut off their ends. Cut a lengthwise *X* on each lime; each knife-stroke should gently penetrate to the flesh of lime. Then, pack salt into the slits. Don't be afraid to use A LOT of salt.

Place the salted limes in a jar and seal it. The limes should be tightly packed. Allow to sit for twelve hours in a cool, dark cupboard, then take the limes out of the jar and squeeze them firmly so their juices release into jar. Repeat this process a few times over 2 or 3 days until the limes are submerged in juice.

Store the limes in a cool, dark cupboard for one month before eating them.

MARMEE'S BIRTHDAY CAKE

MAKES 1 CAKE

Like all food works on *Little Women*, this freshly baked cake was designed to show the March family's love of the outdoors and how they utilized natural beauty to adorn even the simplest cakes to show that love.

The week this scene was filmed was the peak of Boston's autumnal display. My daughter, Charlotte, picked me incredibly bright leaves from trees surrounding Jamaica Plain Pond and the Forest Hills Cemetery. It was a special bonding moment for us and my approach to this cake was to display the gratitude we feel when we are presenting a food gift to someone we cherish. There is a special energy that is achieved when something is displayed with a sentimental spirit.

"Made by" Jo and a group of her young students, this cake was created to resemble that process: bulky, messy, playful. This is a simple chiffon cake recipe with a simple meringue buttercream frosting. I chose to leave the cake whole so it would appear more playful, but know you may cut this cake in half (or use two pans), and then fill it with frosting, jam, or curd to your liking. —Christine Tobin

FOR THE CAKE:

7 large eggs, separated

½ teaspoon cream of tartar or 1 teaspoon lemon juice

1½ cups sugar, divided

2 cups unbleached all-purpose flour

2½ teaspoons baking powder

¾ teaspoon salt

½ cup vegetable oil

¾ cup milk (whole or skim)

2 teaspoons vanilla extract

FOR THE MERINGUE BUTTERCREAM:

¾ cup pasteurized liquid egg whites

6 cups powdered sugar

½ tsp salt

3 cups unsalted butter, at room temperature

2 Tablespoons vanilla extract

1 teaspoon almond extract or ¼ teaspoon Fiori di Sicilia flavoring

To make the cake: Preheat the oven to 325°F. Have ready an ungreased 10 inch tube pan or angel food pan, or two 9 inch round ungreased cake pans. If you're using two round pans, place a rack in the center of the oven; for a tube pan or angel food pan, place a rack just below the center, so the top of the risen cake won't be too close to the top of the oven.

In a large mixing bowl, beat the egg whites with the cream of tartar or lemon juice until foamy. Gradually add ½ cup of the sugar and continue beating until stiff and glossy. Set aside.

Whisk together the remaining 1 cup sugar with the flour, baking powder, and salt and set aside. In a separate bowl, beat the oil, milk, egg yolks, and flavorings until pale yellow. Add the dry ingredients and beat until well blended, about 2 minutes at medium speed using a stand mixer, or longer with a hand mixer.

Gently fold in the whipped egg whites, using a wire whip or cake blender. Be sure to scrape the bottom of the bowl so the batter is well blended. Pour the batter into your pan(s).

If you're using a tube or angel food pan, bake the cake for 50 minutes, then turn up the heat to 350°F for 10 minutes more or until a toothpick inserted into the cake comes out clean. If you're using two 9 inch round cake pans, bake for 40 minutes at 325°F, then 10 minutes more at 350°F or until a toothpick comes out clean.

Cool the cake upside-down in the pan for 30 minutes before using a thin, sharp knife between the cake and the pan to remove it. If you've used a tube pan, set it atop a thin-necked bottle, threading the bottle neck through the hole in the tube. (Cooling with the cake on the bottom and the pan on the top helps keep the sponge light and airy.)

To make the buttercream: Combine the egg whites, powdered sugar, and salt in the bowl of a large stand mixer fitted with a paddle attachment. Mix on low speed, until the sugar is moistened and no dry patches remain. Turn off the mixer, scrape down the sides and bottom of the bowl with a spatula, then turn the mixer to medium speed. Beat on medium for 5 minutes.

After 5 minutes, turn the mixer to medium-low and start adding the room temperature butter, 1 to 2 tablespoons at a time. Once all the butter is incorporated, add the vanilla extract and mix until incorporated. Stop the mixer and scrape down the bottom and sides once more. Turn the mixer on to medium speed and beat the buttercream for 10 minutes. The frosting should be light and fluffy in texture.

To assemble: Place the completely cool cake onto a platter or pedestal. Frost the top of cake with Meringue Buttercream Frosting. (If you have made two cakes, you could fill the layers with more buttercream or with jam or curd.) Adorn with elements of the outdoors for decoration, if you like.

CRANBERRY JAM

MAKES EIGHT 16 OUNCE JARS

It was an unseasonably warm day in New England when we shot this scene. Yellow jackets swarmed my station throughout the day. It's a miracle no one was stung!

This is a very simple recipe for Marmee's Cranberry Jam. Since the scene was set in colder months, cranberry seemed like the perfect New England fruit for Marmee to be making jam with. Tart in nature, once cooked with sugar, the cranberry is reduced to a savory jam for toast or as a condiment for roast meats. —Christine Tobin

10 ounces frozen cranberries	2 cups sugar

In a heavy-bottomed saucepan, combine the cranberries and sugar. Heat over medium-high heat, stirring every few minutes, until the sugar dissolves and the berries release moisture, 12 to 15 minutes. For a smooth texture, carefully transfer the cooled cranberry mixture to a high-speed blender. Secure the lid tightly, and blend on high until the berries and their skins are completely pulverized.

Return the mixture to the heavy-bottomed saucepan and heat over medium heat, stirring every few minutes to prevent scorching. Cook until the mixture thickens into a jam and coats the back of the spoon, without sliding off. This process will take 20 to 25 minutes.

Remove the jam from the heat and let cool slightly. Transfer the warm jam to sanitized mason jars. Refrigerated, the jars will keep for three weeks.

SUGAR AND CINNAMON
APPLE BREAD

MAKES 1 LOAF

This apple bread was prepared as background set dressing for scene 23. Meg is just beginning to learn to cook and bake for her family. I was attracted to this recipe because it forms a "crinkly," messy crust on top, which I thought it would visually emphasize the "roughness" of Amy's amateur baking skills. There are apples galore in New England, and a great way to utilize the March's fruit crops was to prepare various breads, cobblers and pies. This recipe calls for quite a bit of cinnamon and sugar mixture to garnish the warm crust. I consider this sprinkling to be an homage to the Alcott family, who loved granulated sugar and sprinkled it on top of treats, as well as simple fruits, for added sweetness.

Although it was tucked away on the set, this bread quickly became the crew's favorite treat. Our director loved this recipe and I presented her with a bread on our last day of shooting together as a thank-you. Food is love. —Christine Tobin

FOR THE APPLE BREAD:

½ tsp kosher salt

½ tsp baking powder

1 ½ cups flour

½ cup butter, at room temperature

1 cup light brown sugar

¼ cup granulated sugar

½ Tablespoon cinnamon

2 eggs

1 Tablespoon vanilla extract

½ cup milk

1 Granny Smith apple, peeled and finely chopped

FOR THE CINNAMON SUGAR TOPPING:

1 teaspoon cinnamon

1 Tablespoon granulated sugar

For the apple bread: Preheat the oven to 350°F and spray a 9 by 5 inch loaf pan with baking spray. Line the bottom and up the ends of the pan with a strip of parchment paper (for easy removal) and spray again. Set aside.

Whisk together the salt, baking powder, and flour. Set aside.

In the bowl of a stand mixer, beat the butter, both sugars, and the cinnamon for 2 minutes on medium speed, scraping the sides of the bowl as necessary. Add in the eggs and vanilla and continue mixing until smooth, again scraping the sides of the bowl as necessary.

Turn the mixer to low and incorporate the flour mixture and milk in alternating additions, starting and ending with flour. Mix until just combined. Finally, add in the apple and stir until just combined. Pour the batter into the prepared pan.

For the topping: Mix together the cinnamon and sugar and sprinkle on top of the batter.

Bake for 50 to 55 minutes, until the bread is set and a toothpick inserted into the center comes out clean.

Allow the bread to cool in the pan for 10 minutes, and then remove, transferring it to a wire rack to cool completely. Serve warm or at room temperature.

ANATOMY OF A SCENE
THE FIRST WEDDING

"I don't want a fashionable wedding, but only those about me whom I love, and to them I wish to look and be my familiar self."

—MEG MARCH

On a beautiful day in the spring of 1865, full of flowers and sunlight, Meg March marries John Brooke in a simple, emotional ceremony followed by a picnic reception. Laurie dances with Beth, Marmee dances with Father March, and Jo attempts to play the fiddle and quell her profound sadness that Meg has chosen to leave the family nest (a prospect made only more difficult when she learns that wealthy Aunt March has elected to bring Amy with her to Europe and not Jo).

Gerwig staged the wedding outside the March home in Concord, in keeping with the family's love for the outdoors. Although the unconventional festivities weren't necessarily in keeping with social convention at the time, they absolutely reflected the family's counterculture vibe. "The idea of the wedding was a potluck sort of Scandinavian-type of wedding," says prop master David Gulick. "If you had been married into society back then, you would have been presented at a cotillion earlier. They would have arranged the marriage, and you would have been walked down the aisle. This was the opposite of what society was doing."

(Above) Greta Gerwig and crew members watch a take
(Opposite) Marmee, Aunt March, and Mr. Laurence at the wedding of Meg and John Brooke

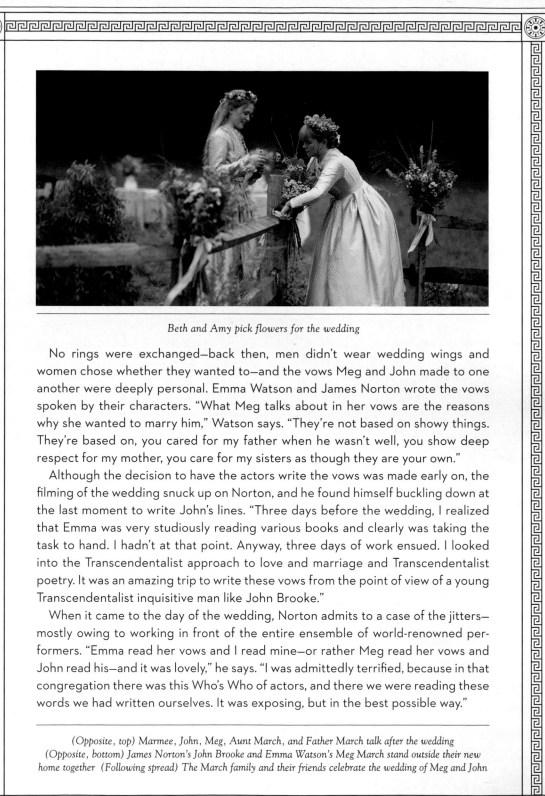

Beth and Amy pick flowers for the wedding

No rings were exchanged—back then, men didn't wear wedding wings and women chose whether they wanted to—and the vows Meg and John made to one another were deeply personal. Emma Watson and James Norton wrote the vows spoken by their characters. "What Meg talks about in her vows are the reasons why she wanted to marry him," Watson says. "They're not based on showy things. They're based on, you cared for my father when he wasn't well, you show deep respect for my mother, you care for my sisters as though they are your own."

Although the decision to have the actors write the vows was made early on, the filming of the wedding snuck up on Norton, and he found himself buckling down at the last moment to write John's lines. "Three days before the wedding, I realized that Emma was very studiously reading various books and clearly was taking the task to hand. I hadn't at that point. Anyway, three days of work ensued. I looked into the Transcendentalist approach to love and marriage and Transcendentalist poetry. It was an amazing trip to write these vows from the point of view of a young Transcendentalist inquisitive man like John Brooke."

When it came to the day of the wedding, Norton admits to a case of the jitters—mostly owing to working in front of the entire ensemble of world-renowned performers. "Emma read her vows and I read mine—or rather Meg read her vows and John read his—and it was lovely," he says. "I was admittedly terrified, because in that congregation there was this Who's Who of actors, and there we were reading these words we had written ourselves. It was exposing, but in the best possible way."

(Opposite, top) Marmee, John, Meg, Aunt March, and Father March talk after the wedding
(Opposite, bottom) James Norton's John Brooke and Emma Watson's Meg March stand outside their new home together (Following spread) The March family and their friends celebrate the wedding of Meg and John

CHAPTER EIGHT

LET'S DANCE

✳

"I can't get over my disappointment in being a girl."

—JO MARCH

Dancers fill the Paris ballroom

In the background, Jo watches Meg at the Gardiner's New Year's Eve party

T'S A FATEFUL DAY IN 1861, NEW Year's Eve, when Josephine March meets Theodore Laurence. Jo accompanies Meg to a ball thrown by the Gardiner family, and while Meg is dancing (in shoes that are far too tight) and delighting in the festivities with her friend Sallie, Jo is desperate to hide. A young reveler has set his sights on dancing with her, and even if the backside of her dress wasn't scorched from standing too close to the fire, she'd still want nothing to do with this unfortunate fellow.

Backing her way out of the party, she finds a secluded area—and her future best friend. The young man who has been away in Europe feels as out of sorts as Jo. He's unfamiliar with American social customs. She's unconcerned with living her life according to them. And just like that, the free spirits feel an immediate, undeniable connection that will shape the course of their lives. While the ball continues nearby, Jo and Laurie share their own lively dance that's as spunky and carefree as the dancers themselves.

"People bring so much of their personality to the way they dance," says choreographer Monica Bill Barnes, who attempted to channel the natural chemistry between stars Saoirse Ronan and Timothée Chalamet into Jo and Laurie's spirited dance. "Saoirse and Timothée travel. They eat up space. That felt so helpful in understanding how to make their duet. I don't think the duet would be relevant to any other two performers, it is so profoundly informed by who they are and who they are together."

A New York–based choreographer and performer and the artistic director of Monica Bill Barnes & Company, Barnes was tasked with creating the steps for the four key dance sequences in *Little Women*: the Gardiner Ball, shot at Boston's Gibson House Museum; the Moffat Ball, filmed at Boston's William Hickling Prescott House museum; the Paris Ball,

(Opposite) Meg dances at the Gardiner's New Year's Eve party

filmed in the Grand Ballroom of Boston's Fairmont Copley Plaza hotel; and the far more informal sequence set at the German beer hall that Jo and Friedrich Bhaer visit after watching a New York performance of *Twelfth Night*.

Barnes had never previously worked in film. Her extensive background is rooted in live performance—she founded her company in 1997 with the mission to celebrate individuality, humor, and the innate theatricality of everyday life. Her work has been performed in unconventional venues in more than eighty cities across the United States, from the Upright Citizens Brigade Theatre to the BAM Howard Gilman Opera House.

But after sitting down with Greta Gerwig (who lives in New York and had attended some of Barnes's performances), she was excited to dig into the challenge of choreographing for film. "I'm a woman who's making work from a perspective that I think is particularly feminine," Barnes says. "*Little Women* is a book that shaped my experience of what it is to be a girl growing into being a woman,

what the possible paths are for women and what they were at that time. I felt inspired by what Greta was interested in, and I felt such a kinship to so much of what about the book influenced and affected Greta."

Barnes immediately recruited choreographer, performer, and rehearsal director Flannery Gregg as the film's associate choreographer to assist her with developing the routines that would be featured on-screen. The two booked time in a New York dance studio to develop a pool of dances that might work for the film.

"Flannery and I began setting polkas to Motown and grand marches to David Bowie, trying to find our own way into these codified period dances," Barnes says. "We wanted a waltz to look like a waltz and a polka to look like a polka, but we didn't want to codify it beyond that. I feel like if I had been in a studio with Flannery trying to do a polka to a polka song, I would have never learned the polka. We ended up doing that to the Cars that has the most perfect polka beat. It's exactly the right tempo."

Assistant choreographer Flannery Gregg with dancers in the Paris ballroom

The idea was to create sequences that felt believable; the March sisters weren't trained dancers, so the movements needed to be correct but looser, more informal. "It is a period piece, but we wanted it to feel contemporary," Barnes says. "We didn't want it to feel stiff and distant. You wanted it to feel like something you could relate to. My goal as a choreographer is to make things that people see themselves in rather than admire for their beauty and grace."

In addition to taking classes in polka and waltz and doing "a lot of YouTubing," Gregg also consulted with dance historian Ken Pierce from the Massachusetts Institute of Technology, who reminded her of important customs related to dance in the 1860s, for example, that the woman's right hand should be extended, not the left. He also worked alongside Gregg to help prepare Florence Pugh and Dash Barber, who played Amy's wealthy suitor Fred Vaughn, for the Paris Ball sequence, in which Pierce appeared as a dancer.

Five different dances were developed for each scene, and the actors had to learn them all during the two-week rehearsal period that took place in Boston prior to the start of filming. They studied the basics of the grand march, in which the dancers walk with a natural stride to moderate tempo music; the galop, a series of slides and steps interspersed with half-turns; and the polka, the fastest and most popular dance of the time.

"We were in a studio working, laying a foundation of how to work together," Barnes says of her time with the cast. "I felt like I could make movement that they would be excited to do and understand intuitively how to perform within their character. It asks a lot of the actors to pick up this skill and weave it into what's happening in their own story lines. I was able to get to know the actors a little bit and understand some things about their personalities and physical impulses.

"People all move the way they move, and no amount of training can change that," Barnes continues. "People bring so much of their personality to the way they dance, so it helped me to have some time with the actors to see how they were. Emma could perfect a step. She has such attention to detail."

For each of the four scenes, the actors would have one five-hour rehearsal period with Barnes and Gregg, during which they would learn all five dances the choreographers had designed for the sequence. The variation was important so that each setting would feel different and distinct. "It can't feel like we're showing four versions of the same thing," Barnes says.

Many of the dances were never used, though. Just two were performed per sequence, and which of them were selected had everything to do with the size and shape of the locations. In the case of the Gardiner and Moffat Balls, specifically, many of the rooms were small, creating an intimate setting where more sweeping movements would have felt out of place. "Once you get into the space, you see how much of a footprint you have to dance in," Barnes says. "You see how many desserts are all around. Some dances wouldn't fit in the space."

At the same time, Barnes and Gregg brought in a group of roughly sixty local Boston dancers to appear as extras in the dance sequences. The choreographers looked exclusively for modern dancers. "If you want the audience to feel like they're watching people at someone's home having a party and dancing, modern dancers have the ability to look like real people more than classically trained ballet dancers or a group of dancers who have studied historically," Barnes says.

A crowd of dancers fill up the room at the German beer hall

The sequence in the German beer hall was the first of the dance-intensive scenes to be filmed; Gregg appeared as one of the dancers. For two choreographers who had never spent time on a film set, the experience was unforgettable. "The German beer hall scene was chaos," Gregg says. "There was this one guy with pitchers of beer coming through the dancers, and there was fake beer on the floor and there was an extra walking in front of two couples who had to connect on the six count. It really felt like people having a good time who were a little bit tipsy, who know these ways of holding their bodies. You have more liberty because of the environment."

From then on, even when things became more formal, Barnes wanted to retain the energetic party atmosphere. To do that, she played the same music on set as she had played when developing the dances with Gregg in the studio—upbeat, contemporary songs like David Bowie's "Modern Love" or the Cure's "Just Like Heaven"—knowing all the while that the music would later be replaced by Alexandre Desplat's orchestral score.

"I almost exclusively work with prerecorded music that's familiar," Barnes says. "In a live performance, it gives the dancers and the audience some sense of being on the same page. Being contemporary people, we respond to music we know more, and I felt like the music anchored the performers in being able to be both responsive and full-bodied, to dive into it. It feels like it brings something fun to the set, in the way that a party should be."

"If David Bowie's 'Let's Dance' is playing," she adds, "you feel like it is a party even though you've been here since four thirty in the morning and your corset is tight."

(Opposite) Jo dances in the German beer hall

CHAPTER NINE

EVER AFTER

✳

"I suppose marriage has always been an economic proposition. Even in fiction."

—JO MARCH

Director Greta Gerwig surveys the scene

Florence Pugh's Amy March and Timothée Chalamet's Laurie in the gardens of a Parisian estate

LOUISA MAY ALCOTT MIGHT HAVE had the idea to make a funny match for Jo, but Greta Gerwig also had thoughts on how to depict the headstrong heroine's romance with Friedrich Bhaer. First off, Friedrich had to be really dashing. "When you've got Timothée Chalamet playing Laurie, you need to not feel like she got the booby prize," Gerwig says. "You don't want to feel like Laurie was the better option. You want to give her someone who feels like she won."

The answer, of course, was Louis Garrel. And although Garrel's Friedrich arrives unannounced at the March home on a random afternoon in 1869, desperately in love with Jo but too retiring to come right out and say so, Gerwig wanted there to be some ambiguity about the culmination of Jo's romance with the professor. So, she came up with a clever twist. As the finale plays out on-screen—with Jo's loved ones encouraging her to follow her

(Opposite) Saoirse Ronan's Jo March contemplates her future

heart and come to terms with her feelings for Friedrich—we also see Jo negotiating with publisher Mr. Dashwood, arguing in favor of leaving the heroine of her book unmarried and meeting with no small amount of resistance to that idea.

As the two story lines intersect, it's difficult not to wonder whether Jo's fairy-tale ending maybe isn't about finding lasting happiness with a husband but instead about realizing her dreams of a literary career. For Gerwig, it's all a matter of interpretation.

"I felt in some ways I was blending what's in the book and what I think [Alcott] would have wanted in the book," Gerwig says. "She didn't think Jo should be married because *she* didn't get married. She thought of herself as a literary spinster, and I think she thought of Jo as an extension of herself. . . . [Alcott] did [have Jo get married], but she had a novel she wrote later where she actually allowed her heroine to be unmarried, and that felt like more of an articulation of what she wanted to do. She was constrained by certain conventions of the time."

Jo discusses her manuscript
with Mr. Dashwood

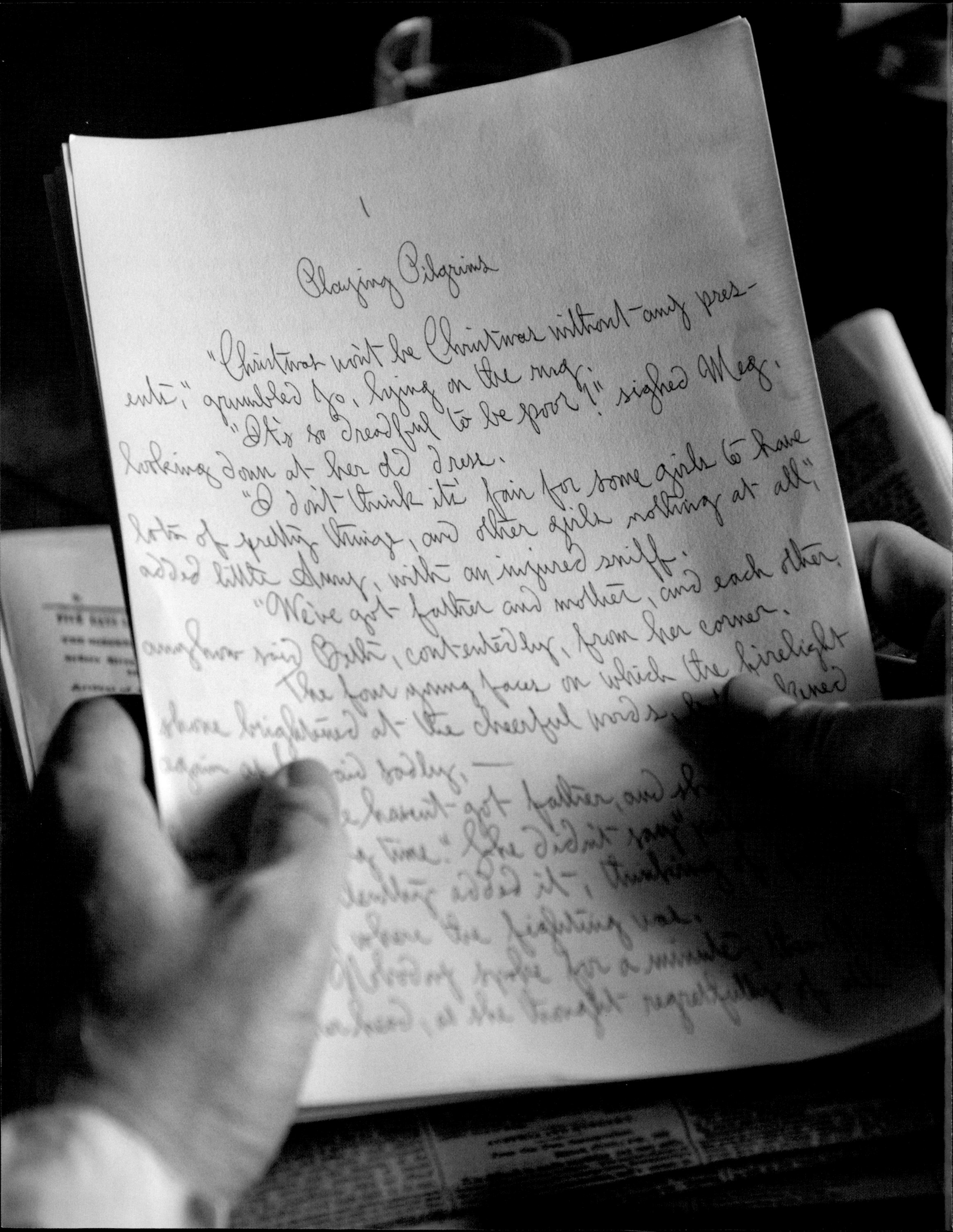

1

Playing Pilgrims

"Christmas won't be Christmas without any presents," grumbled Jo, lying on the rug.
"It's so dreadful to be poor!" sighed Meg,
looking down at her old dress.
"I don't think it's fair for some girls to have
lots of pretty things, and other girls nothing at all,"
added little Amy, with an injured sniff.
"We've got father and mother, and each other,"
anyhow said Beth, contentedly, from her corner.
The four young faces on which the firelight
shone brightened at the cheerful words, but darkened
again as Jo said sadly,—
"We haven't got father, and sh
a long time." She didn't say "p
but each one added it, thinki
father far away, where the fighting was.
Nobody spoke for a minute; th
Meg said, in an altered, at the thought regretfully

Jo opens Plumfield Academy on the estate that she inherited from Aunt March

"I want to do something splendid before I go into my castle, something heroic or wonderful that won't be forgotten after I'm dead. I don't know what, but I'm on the watch for it, and mean to astonish you all some day."

—JO MARCH

Gerwig, of course, had no such constraints, which allowed her to invent a powerful conclusion to the story with enough ambiguity to please both Alcott purists and those who might have wished that the novelist had been able to give Jo the ending she'd intended.

Here, Jo is last glimpsed in 1871 surrounded by loved ones—including Laurie and Amy's

(Opposite) The opening page of Jo's novel, Little Women

infant daughter, Beth—at Plumfield, the estate that she's inherited from Aunt March. She's transformed it into a school for girls and boys of all backgrounds, a progressive place dedicated to equality and creativity. She receives a wrapped package from her publisher, delivered to her by her young nephew, and retreats to her upstairs writing room, a room of her own. She opens the parcel and sees for the first time the proof of her novel, a loving tribute to her family, *Little Women*.

The March family gathers at Plumfield Academy: Laurie comforts his newborn daughter, John and Friedrich share a smile, and Meg, Jo, and Amy present a cake to their beloved Marmee and Father March

FOR VIOLET, MY BRIGHT,
BEAUTIFUL LITTLE WOMAN

—GM

※

Cataloging-in-Publication Data has been applied for and may be obtained
from the Library of Congress.

ISBN 978-1-4197-4068-8

© 2019 Columbia Pictures Industries, Inc. All Rights Reserved
Book design by Headcase Design
Recipes by Christine Tobin
Photos by Wilson Webb
Photos Edited by Roxy Campos

Printed and bound in U.S.A.
10 9 8 7 6 5 4 3 2 1

Abrams Books for Young Readers are available at special discounts when
purchased in quantity for premiums and promotions as well as fundraising
or educational use. Special editions can also be created to specification. For
details, contact specialsales@abramsbooks.com or the address below.

ABRAMS The Art of Books
195 Broadway, New York, NY 10007
abramsbooks.com